Sharon L. Vanderlip, D.V.M.

Yorkshire Terriers

Everything About Purchase, Grooming, Health,
Nutrition, Care, and Training

Filled with Full-color Photographs
Illustrations by Pam Tanzey

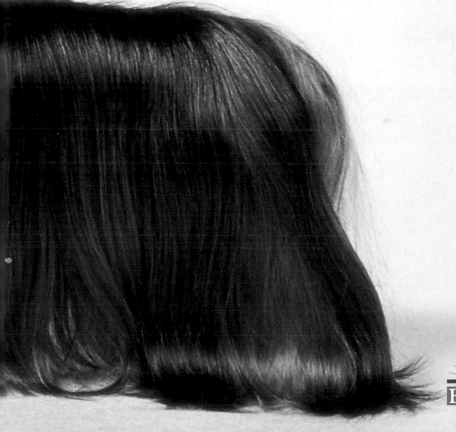

BARRON'S

CONTENTS

YORKSHIRE TERRIER HISTORY

The Yorkshire Terrier is the most popular terrier in the world—and the second-most popular dog breed in the United States. And it's no wonder. This toy terrier with the flowing, silky coat, alluring countenance, and portable size is beautiful, bright, and bonds closely with its owner.

Yorkie Ancestors

The Yorkie shares its ancient ancestry with all dog breeds, tracing back to a creature that looked like a cross between a weasel and a fox, called Hesperocyonines. This primitive animal evolved in North America about 40 million years ago. Hesperocyonines gave rise to many canine species before it became extinct 15 million years ago.

Over the several million years that followed, prehistoric canids eventually developed into the first wild dogs, and later, some differentiated into terrier types. At the time of the Roman invasion of England in 54 BCE, Julius Caesar's legions observed small terriers being used by hunters to chase prey into underground dens and lairs and remain underground to fight and kill their quarry. This instinctive

Yorkshire Terrier, thief of hearts! Meet the world's most popular terrier breed.

terrier behavior is called "going to earth" or "going to ground." The word *terrier* comes from the Latin word *terra*, meaning "earth."

Terrier-type dogs developed into different strains and were highly prized by their owners—and for good reason. They killed rodent pests (such as rats, mice, and gophers) in the home and on the farm. By performing this service, terriers helped prevent food loss by killing vermin that ate and contaminated stored grains and also helped reduce the spread of disease by rodents—in a time before antibiotics! Able hunters of rabbits, squirrels, and other small game, terriers could sometimes help provide for the family dinner table. Terriers provided family entertainment, too, as playful pets in the home, as tough competitors and ratters in the sporting pit, or as loving companion lapdogs in the parlor. Some things never change. Then, as now, terriers were excellent watchdogs. They are very vocal and eager to alert their owners whenever

strangers approach or something is wrong. Best of all, terriers were, and still are, considered part of the family.

Origin of the Breed

One of the best ways to learn accurate details about a breed's history is to research the oldest literature and sources available. This is because the authors were often dog breeders themselves who were alive during the formative stages of the breed and knew breeders and their animals during that historic time. Jessop, author of *Yorkshire Terrier* (1899), says, "Many theories have been advanced as to the derivation of the Yorkshire Terrier, but there is still an element of uncertainty about his composition ... It is most probable that he was obtained by a cross

It's hard to imagine that Yorkies descended from fierce, prehistoric canines. But in your Yorkie's mind, he is just as big and powerful as his ancient predecessors.

between the Clydesdale and Black-and-Tan Terrier, but there are no fanciers now living who can remember him otherwise than as he now is, a blue-and-tan long-haired Terrier, and there are no records which assist us to arrive at any definite conclusion as to what were the crosses originally used in the evolution of a Toy who, whilst he had no doubt many admirers in his early stages, had no chronicler of his beginnings."

Jessop continues, "Authenticated pedigrees of Yorkshire Terriers goes back little further than the early sixties ..." (author's note: 1860s) and asserts, "We may, therefore, with some degree of certainty conclude that the process of selection which has brought the Yorkshire Terrier to his present state of perfection has not extended over at most some fifty to sixty years" (author's note: from about 1840 to 1850).

Of course, the key words here are *process of selection*. A dog breed is not created overnight, and clearly a variety of terrier-type dogs were selected and bred for many years to create the Yorkshire Terrier breed that exists today. We may not have complete written records and descriptions of all the Yorkshire Terrier's ancestors, but we do know something about the kinds of dogs that contributed to the creation of the Yorkshire Terrier breed.

From Scotland to England

It is widely accepted that terrier ancestors of the Yorkshire Terrier originated in Scotland. Terriers were named according to their region of origin, their owners' names, or the type of work they did. They had a variety of names: Waterside, Scotch, Black-and-Tan, Skye, Clydesdale, Paisley, Broken-Haired Scotch, Rosneath, Silk-coated Skye, and Glasgow, to name only a few. Many of these terriers were similar in size, shape, weight, and appearance. Some of them varied in coat type, length, texture, and color. Many of the old terrier breeds no longer exist. Others interbred and were developed into different breeds, for different purposes.

The Waterside Terrier is considered an important ancestor of today's Yorkie. It originated in the shires of Scotland and was recognized for its ratting abilities in the fields, along the canals, and in the ratting pits. In time, the breed disappeared, but before it did, it passed on many of its genes to its descendants, including the Yorkshire Terrier. It is believed that the Waterside Terrier may have contributed the genes responsible for the Yorkie's silky coat texture, blue-and-tan color, small size, and keen ratting ability.

Clydesdale, Paisley, and Skye Terriers were descendants of the Rosneath Terriers. Based on information and descriptions in the old literature, some of these breeds are also considered the foundation breeds of today's Yorkshire Terrier.

Terriers accompanied their Scottish owners when they came to England, seeking work in the mines and textile mills. Breeders from the West Riding and Lancashire areas of Yorkshire, England, are credited with "creating" the Yorkshire Terrier breed, during a turbulent time in history. These areas were adapting to the rapid changes and rise in population brought on by the Industrial Revolution, as well as the hardships and struggles of the Luddite movement. Amidst the turmoil, the Yorkshire Terrier, and many other terrier breeds, originated.

Yorkshire Terrier Foundation Breeds

Rosneath Terrier
Waterside Terrier
Rough-coated Black-and Tan-English Terrier
Paisley
Clydesdale Terrier
Skye Terrier

Jessop suggested that the Yorkshire Terrier was probably obtained by crossing the Clydesdale Terrier (sometimes considered to be the same breed as the Paisley until breeders started breeding these two terrier types to a set standard) and the Black-and-Tan Terrier. He says it was "widely accepted that a variety of terrier breeds were used to create the Yorkshire Terrier."

For a detailed history of the Yorkshire Terrier breed that goes far beyond the scope of this pet manual, *The Complete Yorkshire Terrier*, by Gordon and Bennett, is highly recommended. These Yorkie experts believe the cultivation of the Yorkshire Terrier breed *can* be traced, and they describe in great detail various terriers and their possible contributions to the creation of the Yorkshire Terrier breed.

As we continue to develop new DNA tests for dogs, we are better able to trace their ancestry. For example, recently a common ancestor of many herding breeds was identified by DNA testing for a specific genetic trait (the MDR-1 gene). DNA tests may soon give us more information about the Yorkie's family history.

Pillar of the Breed

The dog acknowledged as the starting point of the Yorkshire Terrier breed, the "original Yorkie," so to speak, is Huddersfield Ben,

The Yorkshire Terrier is the result of interbreeding different terrier types. The Waterside Terrier is credited with giving the Yorkie his silky coat texture, blue and tan colors, and diminutive size.

although at the time Ben was alive, the Yorkshire Terrier was not yet recognized as a breed. In fact, when Ben was exhibited, he was classified as a Broken-Haired Scotch Terrier. Sadly, Ben was run over and killed in a carriage accident in 1871, but in his short life he made an indelible mark on the Yorkshire Terrier breed. We have a good idea of Ben's appearance from photographs taken after he was restored by a taxidermist and displayed in a glass case. But more important, from the old literature we have Ben's pedigree and descriptions of some of his close relatives.

The Kennel Club of England acknowledged the Yorkshire Terrier as a breed in 1886, and in 1897 the first two Yorkshire Terrier champions were titled. The following year the Yorkshire Terrier breed club was formed.

Welcome to America

Americans were in love with Yorkies from the first time the little dogs crossed the Atlantic Ocean and set paws on the continent. As early as 1883, Yorkies appeared in the National American Kennel Club Stud Book, which was taken over by the American Kennel Club (AKC) the following year. Americans were the first to recognize Yorkies as an official breed, to exhibit them in specific Yorkshire Terrier classes, and to award them championship titles. From 1900 to 1920, 45 Yorkshire Terriers became champions in the United States.

As Yorkies rapidly rose in popularity, many people became Yorkie breeders. In 1919, the Yorkshire Terrier Association was formed, but it lasted only a few years. In 1954, the Yorkshire Terrier Club of America was formed.

At the time of its importation, the Yorkie was a sign of status, prestige, and high society to many—and such glamour sold for high prices. Yorkshire Terriers were considered cuddly companions to pamper, groom, carry about, travel with, exhibit, and love. More importance was

Americans were the first to recognize the Yorkshire Terrier as an official breed, exhibit them in specific classes, and award them championship titles.

given to companionship, conformation, and coat quality than to the animal's original purpose: to hunt small game and kill vermin. It was a new world, a new era, and a new lifestyle for the little toy terrier that was destined to rank as the second-most popular breed in America.

Year of the Yorkie—2006!

For more than 10 years, the Yorkshire Terrier consistently ranked among the top 10 most popular breeds in the United States, but 2006 was the Year of the Yorkie. AKC registration statistics show that the Yorkie overtook the Golden Retriever and the German Shepherd in popularity. Promoted from its previous rank of third-most popular breed in the United States, *the Yorkshire Terrier now holds the lofty position of second-most popular breed in the United States.* Close on the tail of America's top-ranking dog, the Labrador Retriever (which has held the number one position since 1991), the Yorkie is poised to one day assume the Labrador's "top dog" rank. Look out, Labs!

Top of the World

The Yorkie is the second-most popular dog in the United States, the most popular toy dog in the United Kingdom, and ranks third in overall breed popularity in the U.K. But love and admiration for the Yorkie doesn't stop there. *The Yorkshire Terrier is the most popular terrier in the world.*

The Yorkshire Terrier Standard

Today's Yorkshire Terrier has not changed much since it was first declared an official breed in 1885. The Yorkshire Terrier still moves in a proud and confident manner. Its moderately long, beautiful, glossy, fine, straight, silky

The Early Years

	America	England
Yorkshire Terriers recognized as an official breed	1885	1886
Yorkies exhibited under the breed name of Yorkshire Terriers	1878	1886
Yorkshire Terriers won a championship title	1889*	1897
Championship title	1905	

*The year 1889 was when the first championship title was awarded after the AKC was established. However, other Yorkies gained championship titles in New York in the early 1880s, and in 1905 the first American-bred Yorkie gained her championship title.

The Yorkshire Terrier has a compact, well-proportioned body. The back is short and level, shoulders and rump are the same height, legs are straight, stifles are moderately bent, and the skull is small and not round on the top.

Feet should be round. The nose, eyelid margins, and toenails are black. A Yorkshire Terrier must not weigh more than 7 pounds (3.18 kg).

A more detailed version of the Yorkshire Terrier Breed Standard may be obtained from the American Kennel Club.

The Yorkshire Terrier's Place in the Dog World

The Yorkie is the world's most popular terrier, so it might come as a surprise to learn that the AKC does not place the Yorkshire Terrier in the Terrier Group (Group IV). The Yorkshire Terrier, with its diminutive size, is a member of the Toy Group (Group V). The toy group consists of several small breeds from a wide variety of origins, appearances, and abilities. What this petite pooch group shares in common is small size and big personality.

coat remains a distinctive feature of the breed, although at the origin of the breed the coat texture was reported to be less silky and more harsh than today's coat.

Coat color is still an important factor in the animal's overall quality. The blue coloration that extends from the back of the neck, over the body to the base of the tail should be a dark, metallic, steel blue, and not silvery. There should not be other colors mingled in the blue hairs. Note: Puppies are very dark at birth. The almost black coloration can take as much as two years to gradually lighten to the desired steel-blue color.

The head, chest, and legs are a deep, rich golden tan. The hair on the head, called the "fall," is long, pulled up, and tied in the center or parted in the middle and tied in two parts. The coat is parted from the base of the skull to the end of the tail, hanging straight and even on each side of a well-balanced and compact body. The head is small and somewhat flat on top. The skull should not be rounded. The teeth meet in a scissors bite or a level bite. Eyes are medium sized and dark. The ears are small, V-shaped, and carried erect. Legs should be straight, with a moderate bend to the stifles.

American Kennel Club Group Classifications

Group I	Sporting Dogs
Group II	Hounds
Group III	Working Dogs
Group IV	Terriers
Group V	Toys
Group VI	Non-Sporting Dogs
Group VII	Herding Dogs
Miscellaneous Class	

Group V—Toys

Affenpinscher	Miniature Pinscher
Brussels Griffon	Papillon
Cavalier King	Pekingese
Charles Spaniel	Pomeranian
Chihuahua	Poodle (Toy)
Chinese Crested	Pug
English Toy Spaniel	Shih Tzu
Havanese	Silky Terrier
Italian Greyhound	Toy Fox Terrier
Japanese Chin	Yorkshire Terrier
Maltese	
Manchester Terrier	
(Toy)	

Yorkies ownership is often associated with prestige, wealth, and fame. Many celebrities have owned Yorkies, and many Yorkies have become celebrities themselves.

Your Yorkie may be a tiny toy, but she's still a terrier—and like all terriers, she can be tough and tenacious. It is her instinctive nature to be as feisty and fearless as her larger cousins. In fact, often the smaller the Yorkie, the tougher she thinks she is!

Famous Yorkies

Yorkies have warmed many laps and brightened many lives, including those of political leaders such as Richard Nixon and entertainers Audrey Hepburn and Joan Rivers. And Yorkies have been entertainers themselves (such as Mignon, on the TV series *Green Acres*). But the Yorkie most deserving of recognition is Smoky, considered by many to be the most famous dog of World War II. She belonged to William Wynne of Ohio, who served in the Air Force and found the 4-pound stray in New Guinea in 1944. Wynne trained Smoky to run communication wire through a culvert under a runway to make it operational during World War II. For her work

she became a war hero. Smoky also won a Best Mascot award. After the war she returned to Ohio with Mr. Wynne, who wrote a book about her titled *Yorkie Doodle Dandy* (1996).

Many Yorkshire Terriers have earned their place in the spotlight: in the show ring, obedience ring, agility, military service, pet-facilitated therapy, and community service. All these animals have done their part to bring attention to the breed and to make the Yorkshire Terrier the most popular dog in the world.

Of course, the biggest celebrity of all is the loyal Yorkie that lives in *your* home and sits on *your* lap. She gives you unlimited and unconditional love. All she needs in return is excellent care—and this book is about how to give your Yorkie the very best care you possibly can—so you both can share many long, happy, healthy years together.

CONSIDERATIONS BEFORE YOU BUY A YORKSHIRE TERRIER

The Yorkie breed has stolen your heart, but don't let it rob you of your senses as well. Don't be an impulse buyer! This dynamic diminutive dog is not for everyone. When it comes to Yorkies, small actually means "really big": big attitude, big responsibilities, and big investments of emotion, time, and money.

There is a lot to learn and think about before you can know for sure whether a Yorkshire Terrier is the right dog for you. And if you decide that a Yorkie is the perfect match for you—get ready! You are about to enjoy many years of love, fun, and companionship from the world's most wonderful and beloved terrier.

There's nothing more lovable than a Yorkshire puppy. But Yorkies aren't for everyone. These tiny dogs have big requirements: lots of tender loving care, constant companionship, regular grooming, and excellent nutrition and health care.

Is a Yorkshire Terrier the Right Dog for You?

The Yorkshire Terrier is a very special dog, and it takes a very special kind of person to understand it, socialize it, train it, and care for it. Yorkies have behavioral and genetic (inherited) terrier traits that are deeply ingrained in this independent, overly confident little canine. After all, the Yorkie is first and foremost a terrier—active, brave, territorial, and a fierce hunter of small prey. In essence, the Yorkie is a big dog in a tiny package. He is still on the lookout for vermin to chase, rodents to kill, and other adversaries to destroy. But in today's

Yorkies are devoted friends and they adore their family. They form intense bonds with one person, usually their caregiver.

world of cities and apartment living, these instincts must be expressed in a different way. These instincts are what drive Yorkies to dig, explore, bark, and sometimes shake, shred, and demolish objects. Yorkies are quick to bark warning alarms, to run and jump (often on and off furniture), and to patrol the premises.

Well known for their big-dog persona, tiny Yorkies think they are giants. An overdose of boldness, combined with their love for adventure, never-ending curiosity, and terrier tenaciousness, can be a recipe for disaster. Your Yorkie can get himself into some potentially dangerous situations, such as a confrontation with a dog 10 times his size. But being a terrier, your Yorkie probably won't back down from danger. Yorkies are not pushovers. They can be fearless to a fault and will not be intimidated.

Yorkies bond very strongly to their owners and do very well in a "one-person" family, so they are ideal for adults, older children, and some elderly people. Yorkies are not suitable for small children because they can injure each

other. Yorkies can be dropped or stepped on by children. Also, Yorkies resent rough handling and may bite if provoked. Although he will adapt to all family members, a Yorkie usually bonds most closely with one person, his caregiver.

Yorkshire Terriers like to dominate. Your Yorkie (we'll call him Dickens) may well decide he is leader of the pack—and the pack includes *you*. If this is the case, you have your work cut out for you. Dickens will resist submitting to you until you teach him in a gentle but firm way that *you* are the boss. The sooner he understands, the better your relationship will be with your small companion, the easier he will be to train, and the less chance there will be for behavior problems.

Yorkies that have not been properly socialized, or that have been overly coddled or not properly trained, may challenge their owners and intimidate them. They may even snap or growl if they don't get their way. This is unacceptable behavior, and preventing it by early socialization and training is much easier, and much more successful, than trying to change bad behavior once it is established.

In many ways, Yorkie puppies are like small children. They are everywhere and into everything all the time. In fact, if it's too quiet in the house, be suspicious. It usually means your Yorkie is getting into trouble.

Your Yorkie may be jealous of the attention you show other people and animals, because he wants *all* of your attention *all* of the time. In fact, Yorkies can be very demanding. They bond closely and form intense relationships with their owners. They don't want to be alone. They are

The Yorkie's beautiful, flowing coat requires daily brushing and lots of grooming.

easily spoiled. Yorkies must receive a lot of socialization, training, and supervision if they are to become good canine citizens. And if Yorkies do not receive fair, firm, consistent discipline when needed, they can develop behavior problems, such as nipping or continual yapping. Misbehavior is one of the main reasons Yorkies end up in animal shelters. If you are going to own a Yorkie, you absolutely must take the time to properly raise and train him.

Yorkshire Terriers are highly intelligent and have excellent memories. They are determined, very active busybodies. These characteristics make training and living with a Yorkie fun, entertaining, challenging, and surprising!

The Commitment to Your Yorkie

Dog ownership is a joy, but it is also a big responsibility. During the years, Dickens will rely on you for love, attention, socialization, training, the right nutrition, regular grooming, and good health care. And with good health care, Yorkies

CHECKLIST

Are You Ready for a Yorkshire Terrier?

1. Would you enjoy the company of a high-energy, inquisitive, adventuresome little dog?
2. Do you have time to take a dog out several times a day and go on daily walks?
3. Do you have time to groom your dog and keep his coat in top condition?
4. Do you have the patience, skill, and time to train a bright little terrier with a mind and will of his own?
5. Can you forgive a little dog for instinctive behaviors, such as digging holes, shredding things, and barking?
6. Can you teach a dog, with kindness, that *you* are the boss, or "pack leader"?
7. Can you "dog-proof" your home and make it safe, to prevent injury and escape?
8. Can you meet the challenges of house training a puppy that might not be so easy to house-train?
9. Can you give enough time and love to a dog that wants to be with you all of the time and may be jealous of attention you bestow on other people or pets?
10. Can you afford food, supplies, grooming, and veterinary care for a Yorkshire Terrier?

If you have answered these questions with a resounding "yes," then get ready to welcome a Yorkshire Terrier into your home. *Your life will never be the same!*

can live up to 15 years, sometimes longer. To put this into perspective, this is almost as long as it takes to raise a child, pay off the home mortgage, or complete a few college degrees. Owning a Yorkie is a commitment for your pet's entire life and a big part of your own life as well.

Don't be misled by the Yorkie's tiny size. Small does not mean cheaper or easier to raise. Yorkies cost just as much as large dogs to own, perhaps even more. Although Yorkies eat less, they have special nutritional needs to meet their high activity level, fast metabolism, and to promote coat growth, so they need the very best food and care you can provide.

The gorgeous, flowing, silky coat for which Yorkies are famous is high maintenance. Regular grooming is an absolute must for every Yorkie and an essential part of skin, coat, and health care. Dickens needs daily grooming, so that means even if you hire a professional groomer most of the time, you still have to participate in the routine grooming. This means taking the time to learn how to do the job right and buying the necessary supplies. *If you cannot commit to regular grooming, then a Yorkie is definitely not for you!*

Yorkies are small, but they are very active and need daily exercise and enough space to run and play. They are not "decorative dogs" that simply sit on plush cushions all day. When you let Dickens outside to exercise and play, plan on exercising as well. Yorkies want someone to play *with* them. They will not exercise on their own. You have to go outside to supervise Dickens's activities anyway, so join him in the fun. It's more healthful for both of you!

A bored, lonely, or shut-in Yorkshire Terrier will soon find some way to entertain himself, and that usually means getting into mischief.

More Important Things to Consider Before You Make the Final Decision

Prepare the Family: Teach children responsibility and respect for animal life. Teach children the correct way to approach and handle your Yorkie so he is not injured from being dropped or stepped on. Be careful that elderly people in the home do not trip and fall over your Yorkie running underfoot.

Allergies: Make sure no one in the family has allergies to animal hair and dander. Consult your physician.

Prepare the House: Select a safe area to house the new arrival. Remove anything breakable, toxic, electrical, or valuable.

Home Schedules: Set aside time to feed, groom, exercise, and play with your Yorkie. Do not leave your Yorkie alone for long periods of time.

Vacations: Leash-train and socialize your Yorkie so he can accompany you on vacation. Otherwise, make arrangements for live-in home care for him (preferable to a boarding facility) and daily exercise.

Expenses: Plan for routine expenses (dog food, health care, supplies, grooming) and unforeseen veterinary medical emergencies.

Prepare the Yard: Make sure the yard is safely enclosed and gates latch securely. Remove poisonous plants. Buy a pool cover to prevent drowning.

Responsible Dog Ownership: License your Yorkie. Enroll in a dog training class. Find a veterinarian. Join a dog club.

Yorkies need space to play and exercise daily.

Prolonged or repeated boredom or isolation can lead to separation anxiety and unwanted behavior such as continual barking, destructive chewing, digging, and soiling in the house. So, when you consider space requirements, remember that companionship, stimulating and fun activities, and daily exercise and outings are just as important.

Yorkies, like all dogs, need good medical care. Basic health care costs for Yorkies, such as physical examinations and vaccinations, are the same as for larger breeds, sometimes more. Yorkies have special health care issues that need to be addressed, such as the need for frequent professional dental cleaning. And because of their tiny size, Yorkies are prone to more medical emergencies than some breeds, such as trauma from being dropped or stepped on, low blood sugar, and hypothermia. In short, veterinary care for a Yorkie costs no less than for any other breed.

Finally, if you are like most Yorkie owners, you will find yourself going on several shopping sprees for Yorkie accessories, such as plush beds, leashes, harnesses, sweaters, hair bows, and toys. Yorkie accessories have a way of turning your wallet into a black hole, so be forewarned!

Caring for a Yorkshire Terrier takes patience, understanding, love, time, and money. So if you can make the commitment, you've made the decision of a lifetime. It's now time to decide when to acquire your new companion.

The Best Time to Acquire Your Yorkshire Terrier

You have made your decision, so now it's time to decide when to introduce a Yorkshire Terrier into your life and home. You can start your search for the perfect puppy now, by contacting breeders and being placed on a waiting list. Don't buy the first puppy you see. Take time to prepare your home for the new arrival

Don't be an impulse buyer! Be sure a Yorkshire Terrier is the right dog for you and that the time is right, before you buy a Yorkie.

and to learn more about the breed, meet breeders, attend some dog shows, join a dog club, and, when possible, visit the puppy you are considering buying. Finding just the right dog takes time, so don't be in a hurry. The perfect match for you is out there, and it's well worth the wait. You'll know him when you find him.

Any major changes in your life, such as relocating, a birth in the family, changing jobs, or taking a vacation, are good reasons to temporarily postpone acquiring your Yorkie. Adding a new pet to your life during this time could mean added stress, rather than fun and enjoyment. Wait until the time is right, so you can spend time with your new little friend and give him the care and attention he deserves. Yorkshire Terriers need a lot of socialization. They thrive on love and suffer when they do not receive enough attention. Yorkies that are left alone for long periods of time are unhappy, lonely, and bored and will eventually get into mischief or develop behavior problems. So wait until you have *lots* of time available before you bring a Yorkshire Terrier into your life.

For Yorkie's Sake!
• Do not buy a Yorkshire Terrier as a gift for someone else. People like to choose their own pets, when the time is right for them.
• Do not buy a Yorkshire Terrier during the holidays. A puppy can be overlooked or neglected during the busy holidays and not get the socialization and attention it needs. It might not be fed on a regular schedule.

- Do not transport a Yorkshire Terrier if it is very young, or if the weather is cold. Shipping and cold stress cause illness, and even death, in young Yorkies.
- Do not buy a Yorkshire Terrier that is less than eight weeks of age; it is too young to leave the breeder. Some states prohibit the sale and transport of puppies less than eight weeks of age.

Other Pets

Your Yorkshire Terrier is full of energy and curiosity. He is smart and has a keen sense of smell. Dickens is interested in meeting all the new members of your family, including your other pets. Play it safe! Make sure introductions are done slowly, safely, and under direct supervision. Never leave any of your pets together, even for a moment, if you are not present.

If you own another dog or a cat, don't expect them to be friends right away. They will be cautious and possibly jealous of the new arrival. A resentful dog's sharp teeth can inflict serious wounds, and eye damage, caused by cat scratches, are common puppy injuries. Even if your pets are happy to have Dickens join the family, be sure that they do not play too roughly. Yorkies may act tough, but they are small and delicate, and their bones are fragile. They can be easily injured. Keep your puppy safe.

A good way to start introductions in the family is to place Dickens in an area of the home where he is safe from other animals but where they can observe and smell each other. A space in the living room or den may be a good place to put a baby-barrier gate to prevent the new arrival from running loose in the house. Be sure your small Yorkie is not able to squeeze through the barrier or become trapped in it.

Always supervise your pets until you are absolutely certain they are compatible. Your Yorkie may be jealous of the attention you give your other pets, so be prepared to lavish him with extra love.

Don't buy collapsing or folding barriers, because Dickens can be caught or crushed in them.

A travel kennel (crate) is an excellent training tool, if used correctly. In the beginning, Dickens should be placed in his kennel only for very short time periods. The kennel should be a safe den to him, not a prison. Your Yorkie should feel happy and secure in his kennel. He should not feel lonely and abandoned.

You may put Dickens in his kennel the first few evenings so that your other animals can approach and investigate but not harm him. Be sure to pay extra attention to your established pets so they still feel special. It will be a real challenge juggling your affections between your pets so that they all feel they have received their fair share!

Keep your Yorkie safely separated from your other pets until you know it is safe for them to be together.

In most cases, animals learn to live together in a household peacefully. However, many Yorkshire Terriers insist on being top dog and will dominate the others, even if they are many times his size.

And what about your other pets that are smaller than Dickens? Look out! Anything smaller than a Yorkie will surely fall prey to it, especially small mammals (such as mice, rats, hamsters, degus, guinea pigs, chinchillas, rabbits) and birds. Even reptiles are not safe. Dickens will follow his instincts and quickly attack, shake, and kill these little creatures. Small pets are no match for your Yorkie's hunting prowess.

Small pets and birds sense when there is a predator in the area. They will be frightened if Dickens approaches their cage. Make sure the lid or door to your small pet's cage is securely fastened. Then place the cage where Dickens cannot find it or reach it.

Good Reasons to Neuter Your Yorkie

Deciding to neuter your Yorkie is one of the most important health decisions you will ever make for him.

Neutering ("spay" for females, "castration" for males) is a surgical procedure in which reproductive organs are removed (ovaries and uterus in the female, testicles in the male) so that the animal cannot reproduce and will not develop cancer in these organs in later years.

Yorkshire Terriers can reach sexual maturity and be able to reproduce as early as six months of age, although at this age they are not completely mature.

Pregnancy can endanger your Yorkie's health. She may even need emergency surgery to deliver her puppies. Neutering your Yorkie, whether male or female, will help prevent health problems, behavior problems, and unwanted pregnancies.

Selecting just one Yorkie can be a daunting task.

The best time to neuter a Yorkie is when it has grown up enough to safely tolerate the anesthesia and surgical procedure. For the female, this should ideally be *before* she has her first estrous cycle ("heat" or "season"). *Spaying a female before she has her first estrous cycle greatly reduces the chance of her developing mammary (breast) cancer later in life.*

Benefits of neutering females
• prevent unwanted pregnancies
• eliminate inconveniences associated with estrus (vaginal bleeding, discharge that stains furniture and carpets and attracts neighborhood dogs)
• prevent cancer of the ovaries and uterus
• help prevent mammary (breast) cancer if spayed before first estrus

Benefits of neutering males
• prevent cancer of testicles and epididymis
• reduce prostate problems
• reduce behavior problems
• reduce tendency to wander
• reduce aggressive behavior

Every Yorkshire Terrier is different, and its medical care should be determined on an individual basis. Consult your veterinarian about the health benefits and possible risks of neutering your Yorkie, the best time to do the procedure, and any other concerns you may have about your pet.

SELECTING YOUR YORKSHIRE TERRIER

Yorkshire Terriers have become victims of their enormous popularity. Because Yorkies are in such high demand, many people raise Yorkies hoping to "get rich quick," without regard for a Yorkie's special needs or genetic makeup. Beware of these sellers. The very best way to find a high-quality Yorkie is to buy from a reputable Yorkie breeder.

Where to Find a Yorkshire Terrier

Buy your Yorkshire Terrier from a reputable breeder. The best way to find a reputable breeder is to contact your local or national Yorkshire Terrier association (see Information) to help you find a respected and knowledgeable Yorkie breeder. The Yorkshire Terrier Club of America can also give you information about Yorkie clubs, shows, and events.

Word of mouth is a good way to find a top breeder. Join a breed, or all-breed, dog club in your area so you can meet breeders, dog trainers, and professional dog show handlers and get their recommendations.

Be wary of sellers advertising in newspapers. Reputable Yorkie breeders have a waiting list for their puppies *before* they are born—often *before* the breeding takes place. Reputable breeders will not be advertising in the newspaper, but "backyard breeders" and "puppy mills" will. Not all breeders advertising in dog magazines and on the Internet will be reputable breeders, either. When you contact breeders from these sources, be sure to ask questions and to get references. A reputable breeder will also ask you questions and ask for references, including your veterinarian's name and phone number.

Be cautious and use good judgment. Talk to the seller to be sure you are dealing with a reputable breeder *before* you visit the puppies.

Buy your Yorkshire Terrier from a reputable breeder. Check the breeder's references and obtain health guarantees in writing.

This healthy Yorkie puppy can fit in an oversized teacup, but an adult Yorkie should weigh more than three pounds and would never fit.

TIP

Tiny Dog, Big Problems

Do not buy "teacup," "miniature," or "doll face" Yorkies, or adult Yorkies weighing 3 pounds or less. These runts usually have health problems, genetic defects, and malformations. They need medical care and have short life spans. They are poor specimens of the Yorkshire Terrier breed. Reputable breeders do not breed or raise them.

Don't let your passion for puppies interfere with your good judgment. Always ask for references and obtain health guarantees in writing. *Decide first on the breeder, then decide on the puppy.*

Puppy, Adolescent, or Adult?

Nothing is cuter than a Yorkie puppy, but puppyhood is brief, so don't base your decision simply on appearance and age. When looking for the ideal companion, the most important considerations are health and personality.

There are many advantages to acquiring your Yorkie (we'll call her Jewel) while she is still a puppy. A Yorkie's personality is well established by the time she is 12 weeks of age. By obtaining Jewel in the early stages of her life, you can positively influence her adult personality and behavioral development. This is much easier than trying to change an established undesirable behavior in an adult dog.

You might find an adolescent or young adult Yorkie that is a perfect match for you. There are many advantages to purchasing an older Yorkie. The breeder will have already socialized and trained her, she will be leash trained and housetrained, and might even know better than to chew your belongings. To be sure that you and Jewel are compatible, request a brief trial period. In general, Yorkies are very adaptable dogs, but it might take a while for your new friend to feel completely at home with a new family and change of lifestyle.

Be prepared to pay more for an older, well-trained Yorkshire Terrier. A lot more time, effort, and expense goes into an adolescent or adult than goes into a puppy.

Picking the Perfect Puppy

Make sure the puppy you choose is healthy. Here is a puppy health checklist to help you in your selection.

Verify that Jewel has been registered with the kennel club and ask for a copy of her registration papers. If they are not yet available, ask for a copy of her parents' registration papers. The breeder can also provide you with a copy of Jewel's pedigree.

Ask the breeder if Jewel's parents have additional certifications.

Important questions to ask the seller:

1. What kind of health guarantee does the breeder offer?

2. Have the pups been examined by a veterinarian?

3. Are the pups purebred and registered with the kennel club?

4. How old are the pups, and which one(s) is available?

5. Have the pups received any vaccinations, and if so, which ones?

6. Have the pups been tested or treated for parasites?

7. Have the pups received any basic training (house-training, leash training) and are they well socialized?

8. What kind of food are the pups eating?

9. Does the breeder have any special information or advice to offer about the puppy you selected?

10. Ask to see the puppies' parents.

Male or Female?

Both male and female Yorkshire Terriers make wonderful companions. Every Yorkie has its own unique personality, so it's not accurate or fair to

make a generalized statement about whether males or females have the best temperaments or make the best pets. It all depends on your personal preferences and your Yorkie's environmental influences, genetic traits, learned behaviors, and training.

CHECKLIST

Yorkie Puppy Health

✔ **Attitude:** Healthy, alert, playful, inquisitive, eager to greet you

✔ **Eyes:** Bright; clear; free of discharge, tearing, and staining

✔ **Ears:** Clean; free of parasites, dirt, and wax; no head shaking or scratching

✔ **Mouth:** Gums bright pink, teeth properly aligned

✔ **Skin and Coat:** Healthy, glossy, clean, with no parasites or sores, no mats or knots, no soiling or diarrhea under the tail

✔ **Tail and Dewclaws:** Dewclaws have been removed and tail has been docked* (top two-thirds removed)

✔ **Body Condition:** Full body, not too thin, and does not have a distended or bloated belly

✔ **Movement:** Normal gait for a puppy; moves freely and willingly; no limping, hopping, or skipping

*These procedures are done at three to five days of age. If done later in life, they require anesthesia and pain relievers. If you are not going to show your puppy, tail docking is not necessary. Tail docking is not permissible in some countries that consider the procedure unnecessary and inhumane.

Male Yorkies can be very territorial and "mark" their territory by lifting a leg and urinating on it—frequently. Neutering at a young age may help reduce this tendency. Males can also take longer to house-train than females. Female Yorkies try just as hard as males, perhaps harder, to be the "alpha" or dominant animal. Regardless of their sex, Yorkies think they are big and tough, and they act like it. After all, they are terriers through and through!

One or More?

If you are thinking of raising Yorkshire Terriers in the future, you will, at some time, want to buy another Yorkie—or two, or three. Discuss your intentions with the breeder. Ask for help in selecting the best animals. Learn everything you can about the breed and then invest in the best animals available. You will need the help of experienced breeders to embark on this very challenging endeavor.

If you are thinking about owning more than one Yorkie as a companion, there are some advantages and drawbacks to consider:

Advantages

• More fun and surprises.

• You will not be alone and will always have Yorkie companionship.

• Yorkies can keep each other company and play together.

• Yorkies are small enough that you can take them on walks together.

• Yorkies do not eat a lot, so feeding two Yorkies will not cost a lot more.

Drawbacks

• More time and work: training, grooming, cleaning.

• More expense: health care, supplies, accessories.

• Yorkies may be jealous of each other, or they may bond more closely to each other than with you.

• Yorkies can reinforce misbehavior in each other, including house-training problems.
• Yorkies may need different diets and may have to be separated when fed.

Show Dog or Companion Only?

A Yorkshire Terrier destined for the show ring must adhere closely to the breed standard and be an outstanding representative of the breed. A companion Yorkie may have minor imperfections with regard to the high conformation standards of a future champion but be wonderful in all other respects. Usually the differences between a champion and a nonchampion Yorkie are obvious only to the trained eye of a dog show judge or an experienced breeder. They in no way diminish the animal's value as a loving member of the family.

If you are bitten by the show bug and must purchase a show dog, be prepared to pay more for it than you would for a pet-quality companion. And if you buy a puppy as a "show prospect," there is no guarantee that it will turn out to be a champion, even if its parents are champions. Even the loveliest puppy can change as it grows up and goes through

Decisions, decisions! Whichever puppy you choose, it will be hard to leave the others behind.

developmental growth phases. Your pup may not reach the show potential you had hoped it would. If you really want to win in the conformation ring, consider buying an adult Yorkie

━━━━ T I P ━━━━

Leave Dog Breeding to the Experts!

Many people make the mistake of thinking dog breeding is easy and that they can make money by breeding their pets and selling the puppies. They are wrong. Dog breeding is a labor of love. It is *not* profitable if it is done right! Good nutrition, medical care, vaccinations, medications, cleaning, training, and supplies are expensive. Feeding, cleaning, and taking care of the mother and puppies is hard work. Yorkshire Terriers have health and genetic issues to consider. Pregnancy and whelping can risk the health of the mother, she may require emergency surgery, or she may produce sick or defective puppies. *If you are serious about breeding Yorkies, learn from the experts and don't start breeding Yorkies until you are an expert yourself.*

Have your Yorkshire Terrier neutered!

that has already been successful at the shows. It will be hard to find one for sale, but once in a while a great opportunity presents itself. Be prepared to pay for it.

Age and Longevity

Small breeds live longer than large breeds, and Yorkshire Terriers live a long time! With good nutrition and excellent care a Yorkie may live up to 15 years or more. So choose your new companion wisely. You and your Yorkie are going to be together for many years.

Important Documents

Before you complete the sale, check your future Yorkie's health records, registration papers, pedigree, health guarantees, and sales contract. Ideally your puppy should have a health certificate signed by a veterinarian saying that the puppy has been examined and is in good health and able to travel. Dates of vaccinations, medications, and microchip identification number should all be noted on the health certificate.

A lot of the fun of owning a purebred Yorkie is showing it off and participating in fun dog activities. Official registration with the American Kennel Club (AKC) proves that your Yorkie is really a Yorkie and allows your dog to compete in AKC dog sports and competitions.

Full Registration

This type of registration is for show dogs and breeding animals. It allows for participation in AKC conformation class, competitions, and events, and makes it possible to register future offspring of the animal with the AKC.

Yorkie Quick Reference Chart

	High	Moderate
Grooming Needs	✗	
Intelligence, Trainability	✗	
Watchdog Ability	✗	
Protective, Territorial	✗	
Bonds with One Owner	✗	
Energy Level	✗	
Mind of Its Own	✗	
Ease of Spoiling	✗	
Challenges Authority	✗	
Friendliness (with Strangers)		✗

═CHECKLIST═

An Informed Owner
✔ Begin the search for your Yorkshire Terrier by contacting the Yorkshire Terrier Club of American and local breed clubs, visiting dog shows, and contacting reputable, respected breeders.
✔ Learn as much as you can about the Yorkshire Terrier breed, talk to breeders, and ask them questions.
✔ Decide whether to purchase a puppy, adolescent, or adult Yorkie.
✔ Remember that health and personality are the key considerations.
✔ Obtain all relevant documents *at the time of purchase.*

Sometimes an unfortunate Yorkie needs help. If you are prepared to accept the challenges of adopting a rescue Yorkie, contact a Yorkie rescue group (see Information).

Limited Registration

Dogs that are sold as pets, and not for show or breeding, should be sold with a limited registration. Dogs with limited registration cannot be used for breeding, and if they are bred, their offspring cannot be registered with the AKC. Dogs with limited registration cannot compete in conformation classes, but they can compete in other AKC events, such as obedience and agility. Only the dog's breeder (not the owner) can change a dog's status from limited registration to full registration.

Help! What About Rescue?

Many Yorkies end up in animal shelters or with rescue groups. Most are adults that have been relinquished because of behavior problems, usually related to failure to be house trained. Barking, destructive behavior, separation anxiety, and biting are also high on the problem list. Many of these Yorkies also have health and genetic problems. Some Yorkies have simply been abandoned because their original owners didn't have time for them.

Giving a Yorkie a second chance in life is challenging, but can be very rewarding. If you have the patience, time, knowledge, and finances to provide a home for a Yorkie in need, the Yorkshire Terrier Club of America and other groups (see Information) can put you in touch with a rescue coordinator.

AT HOME WITH YOUR YORKSHIRE TERRIER

You have found the perfect Yorkie and now it's time to bring him home. Everything must be perfect for the new arrival so he will feel safe and secure!

Yorkshire Terriers, especially baby Yorkies, like to feel comfortable and safe. Yorkies are quick to adapt, and you can make the transition period easy and stress-free for your puppy and yourself by being well prepared before bringing your new little friend home.

Your Yorkie Comes Home

The first step in preparing your Yorkie for the trip home is to get him used to a travel kennel. This is usually done by the breeder, in anticipation of your puppy's future trip home with you. Most breeders introduce their puppies to a travel kennel when they are very young, so they can play and sleep in it and

Welcome home! Joining a new family is a big change for a little Yorkie. Give him a warm, cozy place where he will feel safe while he adapts.

use it as a "den." If Dickens is already used to a travel kennel, the trip home will be safe and pleasant.

If he is not used to traveling, the ride home might be filled with mournful whimpering or shrill yapping. Don't give in! This first trip will set the "rules of road" for all the years to follow. If you hold Dickens on your lap, he will expect to be outside the travel kennel on every trip. In fact, he will demand it! A dog that is loose in the car is a distraction and can cause an accident, or be tossed about and seriously injured in an accident.

Leave your Yorkie in the travel kennel where he is safe while you are driving or traveling in the car.

If Dickens feels queasy, he may drool, vomit, or defecate, so be sure to bring along plenty of disposable towels and a plastic bag. Carsickness is common in young Yorkies. Dickens will outgrow his carsickness faster if you take him on short car

═══ T I P ═══

Road Trip Advice

Allow your pet to relieve himself before starting out on a trip. Place a favorite toy or blanket in the travel kennel that will make him feel secure, so he can relax or sleep. To reduce chances of carsickness and vomiting, withhold food one hour before travel.

trips on a regular basis. Reward him with a small treat and play with him after each trip.

When you first bring Dickens home, he will be tired from the trip and all the excitement of new people and a new environment. Give him a little quiet time and a drink of water. Yorkie puppies have fast metabolisms. They burn up calories very quickly and they tire quickly. They need a lot of sleep. If there are children in the

home, teach them to respect Dickens's naptime. Children's shrill voices and sudden movements can startle a tiny puppy.

It is very important to teach children in the home the proper way to lift and handle Dickens, by gently putting one hand under his chest and the other under his hindquarters for support. Small children should remain seated, preferably on the floor, when petting or handling a Yorkie, so they do not drop or injure the animal.

Supervise children at all times when they are holding a Yorkie!

Most Yorkie injuries—broken bones and head trauma—are caused by being dropped or stepped on.

Never lift a Yorkie by the scruff of the neck or by the limbs.

Naming Your Yorkie

Your Yorkie's personality will shine through, and it won't be difficult for you to think of the perfect name that matches his personality. It is easiest for dogs to recognize names with two syllables. Names ending in a vowel sound are easy for dogs to identify, such as Loki or Risa. Trainers sometimes recommend using two-syllable names to help avoid confusing dogs when you give one-syllable commands, such as *sit, stay,* and *down.* However, Yorkies are very bright. They can easily tell the difference between a name and a command—the question is whether the Yorkie will choose to *obey* the command!

A travel kennel should be large enough for your Yorkie to comfortably and easily stand, sit, and turn around. Remember to give your Yorkie water after every trip.

Yorkie Collars

Yorkies are so small that cat collars may be safer and more suitable for them than buckle dog collars. For Yorkies that have tracheal collapse problems, harnesses are recommended. Check your pet's collar daily to be sure it fits properly and is not breaking the hairs on the neck.

If you cannot think of a good name, dog name books are available that list hundreds of names and their meanings (see Information). It won't take long for your Yorkie to learn his name. In fact, he will not only know when you are talking *to* him, but will also know when you are talking *about* him! Once Dickens knows his name, you can get his attention and start communication—the first step in his lifelong training.

Housing Considerations

Ever since their early history, Yorkshire Terriers have been indoor dogs. They may have spent hours in the fields hunting and killing vermin, but when they were not working, they were safely tucked away in the home. In fact, tucked away is a good way to describe their housing. In England during the 1800s, Yorkies were housed in boxes kept under the table, or in kitchen cupboards. The cupboard doors were replaced with wire mesh or bars so that the dogs could observe family activities in the kitchen. Sometimes the animals' quarters were stacked or tiered. Today's Yorkie is much more

Yorkie Necessities

✔ Travel kennel
✔ Comfortable sleeping quarters and dog bed or big pillow cushion
✔ Food and water dishes, water bottles with sipper tubes
✔ High-quality puppy/dog food recommended by the breeder or veterinarian
✔ Lightweight cat collar
✔ Dog harness for walks (ideal for safe, fast pickup in case of emergency)
✔ Leash (retractable-style is *not* recommended for training)
✔ Sweater for warmth
✔ Grooming and dental supplies (see Grooming Your Yorkie)
✔ First aid kit
✔ Exercise pen (X-pen), safety gate, or other safe, escape-proof enclosure
✔ Safe, chew-proof toys

fortunate. He is often given full run of the house and allowed to sit on the furniture, and if he is especially spoiled, he may even sleep in his owner's bed!

When Yorkies are not outside exploring, taking a walk, or playing, they should always be housed inside where they are safe and can be supervised.

Location

Before you bring Dickens home, decide on a place to house him (an X-pen, or an area blocked off from, but near, the family room or living

Most Yorkie injuries are caused by being stepped on or being dropped. Teach everyone in the family the correct way to hold your Yorkie.

Convenient Housing Options

Travel Kennels: Ideal for small doghouse, lightweight, easy to clean and disinfect, well ventilated, draft-free, private.

Exercise Pens (X-pens): Available in a variety of sizes, attachments for dishes and bottles, optional fitted wire tops.

Safety Gates: Close off areas and stairways to prevent escape or injury. Do not use accordion-folding barriers or gates that can collapse, fold, trap, and injure Yorkies.

Bedding: Bedding should be natural material (cotton, wool). Some synthetic materials or bedding containing cedar shavings can cause skin and respiratory allergies.

Once you have selected an area to house Dickens, take him there to explore, relax, eat, drink, and sleep. Feed him a little treat and spend time visiting with him. Of course, Dickens will complain when you leave him and will want to be released to have full run of the house, but don't give it to him! Your Yorkie

Yorkie puppies tire easily and need lots of rest. Make sure your puppy gets the sleep he needs.

room) where he is safe and you can observe him. Choose wisely, because this area may eventually become Dickens's permanent housing and sleeping quarters. Yorkshire Terriers want to be the center of attention. They also want to be in the center of all activities. But being everywhere all the time is not safe, especially for a new puppy. And just like people, Yorkies need privacy and quiet time. A travel kennel is ideal for use as a den and will give Dickens a sense of security without isolating him from the family.

must learn house rules and be socialized and trained before it is safe for him to expand his boundaries in your home.

Exposure to various sights, sounds, smells, activities, and people are all an important part of Yorkie socialization. Dickens doesn't know the rules yet, so make sure his space is in an area where he cannot chew electrical wires, baseboards, or furniture, and cannot urinate on the carpet.

If you have acquired an older Yorkshire Terrier, try to duplicate the previous housing situation as much as possible to reduce the stress of changing environments.

Safety First

Many of the things you love most about your Yorkie—his tiny size, high activity level, and curiosity—also make him accident-prone. Before your Yorkie comes home, you must do a safety check and "Yorkie-proof" your home by removing all potential hazards from your diminutive friend.

Make sure your home is safe before you let your Yorkshire Terrier go exploring.

Supervise your Yorkie at all times.

Household Cleaning Products and Chemicals

Because your Yorkie is so tiny, it takes only a tiny amount of toxic substances to kill him. Keep cleaning products and chemicals out of your pet's reach.

Antifreeze

Antifreeze (ethylene glycol) is a common cause of animal poisoning. It can be found on garage floors and has a sweet taste that attracts animals. A very small amount can cause permanent, severe kidney damage. Survival depends on an early diagnosis. Keep Dickens out of the garage.

Rodent Poisons and Snap Traps

Rodent bait is deadly for all animals. If Dickens consumes rodent bait or eats a poisoned rodent, he will be poisoned as well.

If you have set snap traps in your house or garage, remove them. They can easily break a Yorkie's tiny toes or injure a nose.

Electrical Shock

Make sure your Yorkie cannot reach or chew on electrical cords. Electrocution from gnawing on an electrical cord could cost Dickens his life and possibly cause an electrical fire.

Kitchen and Appliances

Many pets have been seriously burned by hot liquids spilled from pots on the stove. Yorkies

Make sure your Yorkie does not chew on electrical wires.

Lawn and garden fertilizers, and cocoa mulch, are poisonous to dogs. Most ornamental plants are also poisonous. Limit plants in your home to non-poisonous varieties and make sure that your backyard is safe for your Yorkie.

Injuries

Yorkie ownership means learning to shuffle your feet! One of the most common Yorkie injuries is broken bones resulting from being accidentally stepped on by a family member. Dickens can dart out from under the furniture and be underfoot before you know it. If you try to sidestep him, you can also be injured if you lose your balance or trip and fall.

Another common Yorkie injury is trauma from being dropped. Even a few feet is a sky-dive fall for a tiny Yorkie, and those delicate bones break easily. Handle with care.

Poisonous Plants

Many, if not most, ornamental plants are toxic to animals. Yorkshire Terriers have a natural instinct to dig and explore. Keep house-hold plants out of reach, and limit home and garden plants to nontoxic varieties.

Fertilizers and Mulch

Lawn and garden fertilizers are poisonous to dogs. Cocoa mulch is very toxic to dogs. It contains theobromine, the same methylxan-thine found in chocolate. Do not use cocoa mulch or fertilizers in areas of your yard where Dickens plays.

are active and constantly underfoot, so don't let Dickens run around your feet in the kitchen while you are cooking. You could spill something on him, he could be stepped on, or he could trip you.

Doors

Make sure all doors to the outside and to the garage are closed. If Dickens escapes outdoors, he can become lost, stolen, hit by an automobile, or injured by wildlife (coyotes, raccoons, hawks) and neighborhood dogs.

The garage is a dangerous place for a Yorkie. Dickens could gain access to stored toxic chemicals or be hurt by sharp tools.

Be careful when closing doors. Many Yorkie injuries and broken bones are caused by being caught in closing doors.

Foreign Objects

Dogs explore with their mouths and swallow unusual things. If an object is within Dickens's reach, he will sample it. Make sure small balls, children's toys, rubber bands, paper clips, pens, coins, and all other unsafe objects are out of reach. Pennies contain high levels of zinc and can cause zinc poisoning. Be sure that the toys you purchase are safe toys that cannot be chewed or broken down into smaller pieces and swallowed. Avoid toys with small pieces, bells, or whistles that may be a choking hazard.

Garbage

"Garbage poisoning" is common and can cause death. It is caused by spoiled and decaying foods that are contaminated with bacteria that produce toxins and cause poisoning. In addition, dogs that rummage through the garbage often eat paper wrappers, plastic wrap, aluminum foil, bones, and other objects that can cause intestinal obstruction. Keep your Yorkie out of the trash!

Paper Shredders

Turn your paper shredder off when you are not using it. A curious Yorkie can lose his tongue if he licks a paper shredder that is set on "automatic feed."

Candies, Medicines, and Foods

Candies and medicines are dangerous for Yorkies. An overdose of common medicines, including aspirin and ibuprofen, can be fatal. Chocolate contains a methylxanthine substance (theobromine) similar to caffeine that is toxic to dogs. Some artificial sweeteners, found in human foods and candies, are toxic for dogs. Hard candies can become lodged between the teeth at the back of the jaw or be a serious choking hazard.

Grapes and raisins are toxic to dogs and cause acute kidney failure. Macadamia nuts are also poisonous to dogs.

Identification

As soon as your Yorkshire Terrier is big enough, have him permanently identified. If Dickens ever becomes lost, your chances of

Your Yorkie puppy must stay in a safe, secure area and be trained before he can have full run of your home.

being reunited are very slim without proper identification. Ninety percent of all lost family pets are unidentifiable, and 70 percent of these animals never return home. Annually 20 million lost American pets are euthanized. Don't let Dickens become one of the statistics.

Microchips

One of the best forms of animal identification is a microchip. A microchip is a tiny transponder about the size of a grain of rice. It is implanted under the skin quickly and easily by injection. The microchip identification numbers are read by a handheld scanner. Microchips are safe, permanent, and tamper-proof. The entire identification procedure takes only a few seconds. Scanning is absolutely painless and is accurate.

A central computer registry records the animal's identification number and owner information. Lost animals can be identified at animal shelters, humane societies, and veterinary offices.

Microchip price, including implantation, is modest (currently $30). In addition, the price for lifetime enrollment in the American Kennel Club Animal Recovery database is currently only $12.50.

Microchip identification is one of the best things you can do for your Yorkie.

Collars and Harnesses with Nametags

Nametags are an excellent form of identification. Many pet stores offer on-the-spot nametag engraving. Tags are easily visible and let others know your lost companion has a family. *Be sure to keep a current phone number on the tag.*

Tattoos

Tattoos are a good form of identification because they are visible and permanent. Yorkies are so small that identification numbers may have to be tattooed on the belly, rather than the usual location of the inner thigh. You can register Dickens's tattoo number with the American Kennel Club Animal Recovery program. There are also tattoo registries (see Information).

If you are having Dickens neutered in the near future, ask your veterinarian about tattooing him at the same time, while he is under anesthesia for the surgical procedure. Your veterinarian may also recommend tattooing Dickens under light sedation.

House-training Your Yorkie

Behavior problems are the biggest reasons owners relinquish their Yorkshire Terriers to animal shelters and rescue groups, and house-training failures top the list.

Yorkies are very smart. They are also very clean. So why does it take some Yorkies a long time to become fully house-trained? Because some Yorkie owners do not know the correct way to house-train their puppies!

The secrets to successful Yorkie house-training are patience, diligence, attentiveness, consistency, making sure your puppy gets to the right place at the right time, and lots and lots of praise.

Your Yorkie has a very small urinary bladder and intestinal tract, so there is very little holding space. *Yorkie puppies must eliminate frequently, at least once every two to three hours.*

Give Dickens several opportunities throughout the day to relieve himself, so that he does not accidentally soil in the house or develop bad toilet habits. Take him to the same spot every time. When you need to get some sleep or be away from the house for a while, confine him to an X-pen and spread newspapers or "wee pads" (from the pet store) on an easy-to-clean floor (such as tile or linoleum). You can also train your puppy to use a litter box. Give him a shallow litter box filled with absorbent dog litter from the pet store, or strips of sod from the

═══ TIP ═══

House-training
1. Start house-training your Yorkie puppy the day he arrives—it is never too early.
2. Let your puppy out several times a day to eliminate, at least every two to three hours.
3. Let your puppy out to eliminate first thing in the morning, after every meal, after drinking, after naps, and as late as possible in the evening.
4. Never scold your Yorkie puppy if he has an accident.
5. Praise your Yorkie profusely when he does the right thing.
6. Be patient, understanding, kind, firm, and consistent in your training.

Yorkie puppies have to urinate and defecate frequently. Keep your puppy in a designated area while he is being house trained. Use a safe baby gate that will not fold, collapse, or injure him.

nursery. *Be sure the sod does not contain fertilizer.* The box sides should be low enough for Dickens to enter and exit easily. Place a very small amount of Dickens's excrement in the box to give him the idea. Put him in the box when he shows signs of impending elimination.

Until Dickens is fully vaccinated, do not take him outside where other dogs have gone. He may contract diseases or parasites.

A travel kennel is a valuable house-training tool, as long as it is not misused. Yorkies hate to soil their living quarters. If Dickens is in his travel kennel, he will hold himself as long as he possibly can. This can be useful if you need to leave the house for 20 to 30 minutes. Let him out immediately upon your return and take him to the right spot to do his business.

Yorkies gain more control over their bodily functions with time. When Dickens is an older puppy, you can put him in the travel kennel late at night and let him out first thing in the morning. Be sure to get up early. It's unfair for you to sleep in while your puppy is miserable with a full bladder.

Never use the travel crate for long-term confinement.

Until your Yorkie is house-trained, limit his access to your home. When Dickens is not with you, confine him to an X-pen or other safe enclosure, so he does not accidentally soil in the house.

Never discipline a Yorkie by shouting at him, shaking him, or striking him. This very cruel punishment can injure him physically and emotionally. Always be kind, patient, and consistent in your training and give your puppy lots of praise and the love he deserves.

In spite of your diligence, there will be some "accidents" before Dickens is fully house-trained. Keep in mind that these are not intentional. *Do not punish, strike, or shake your Yorkie. Do not raise your voice.* Simply say "No" and put him in the spot he is supposed to use. Then clean the soiled area well so he will not be attracted to it later. *Use positive reinforcement only. Praise your Yorkie profusely and give him a treat when*

TIP

Accidents

Most elimination "accidents" occur because the owner did not pay attention to the puppy's behavior. Other accidents occur because *the puppy did not*

- have enough opportunities to go outside
- know where he should do his eliminations
- know how to ask to be let outside

If a Yorkie (puppy or adult) is house-trained and starts having accidents in the house, this could be a sign of medical problems such as a bladder infection. Consult your veterinarian right away.

he does the right thing. Be kind and patient—he is just a baby.

Watch your puppy closely for signs of impending urination or defecation so you can take him outside in time and prevent another accident. Signs include

- sniffing the ground
- pacing
- circling
- whining
- crying
- acting anxious

Act quickly as soon as this behavior begins, or you will be too late!

Your Yorkie will need to urinate immediately after waking up from a nap, or after eating a meal or drinking, so in these instances, take him directly outside without waiting for signs. Always lavish praise on him for his performance.

Dental Care

Yorkies need daily tooth brushing, or they will quickly accumulate tartar and plaque on their teeth. Tartar and plaque start with bacterial growth and food debris on the dental surface. These harden into a brown coating, starting at the gum line. Periodontal disease develops and causes swollen, painful, bleeding gums and tooth loss. Bacteria present in the mouth and gums enter the bloodstream and can grow on the heart valves or infect the kidneys and other organs of the body.

Bad breath is not normal for a dog. It is a sign of a health problem, including dental disease. If Dickens has bad breath, consult your veterinarian. He may need to have an ultrasonic dental cleaning and polishing and antibiotics.

The best way to prevent dental disease is to brush your Yorkie's teeth daily. Start when he is a puppy. The baby (deciduous) teeth will have fallen out by the time he is an adult, but they are good for practice and training. By the time your Yorkie's adult teeth are in, he will be used to the daily routine.

Purchase a soft-bristle toothbrush and dog toothpaste (dentifrice) recommended by your

Check your Yorkie's teeth regularly. Regular brushing will help reduce plaque and tartar accumulation on your Yorkie's teeth.

veterinarian. Do not use human toothpaste. Many human products contain spearmint or peppermint. These substances make dogs salivate (drool) and upset their stomachs.

Brushing the Teeth

Start with the upper front teeth (incisors), brushing down and away from the gum line, and proceed back to the premolars and molars on each side of the mouth. You may also brush in a gentle, circular motion. Pay special attention to the upper canine teeth and molars, as plaque and tartar accumulate faster on these teeth. When you brush the bottom teeth, start with the incisors and work back to the molars, brushing up and away from the gum line. Spend about one minute on the upper teeth and then praise Dickens for his good behavior. Repeat the procedure on the bottom teeth for one minute and follow again with profuse praise.

Good home dental care is a necessity, but it is not a replacement for veterinary dental visits. Even with the best of care, most Yorkies need routine professional dental cleaning and polishing.

TIP

A Beautiful Smile

Retained baby teeth are common in Yorkies. If the deciduous teeth do not come out when the adult teeth grow in, teeth are overcrowded in the mouth and dental problems result. Retained deciduous teeth must be extracted!

Toenails

Nail trimming prevents the nails from snagging or tearing. If the nails become overgrown, they can interfere with movement and the ability to walk correctly. In severe cases, overgrown toenails can curve under and pierce through the flesh of the foot pads.

Cutting Yorkie toenails takes practice because their toenails are black. You cannot see the quick (where the blood supply begins).

To check if Dickens needs a nail trim, stand him on the grooming table. None of the nails should touch the surface of the table. Notice that each toenail curves and tapers into a point. Trim only the curved tip of the nail.

Most Yorkshire Terrier experts prefer guillotine-style clippers for adult dogs. To use these, place the toenail inside the metal loop, aligning the upper and lower blades with the area you wish to cut, and squeeze the clipper handles. If you accidentally cut too close, you can stop the bleeding by applying styptic powder or gel (available from your veterinarian or pet store) or by applying pressure with a clean cloth to the toenail for five minutes.

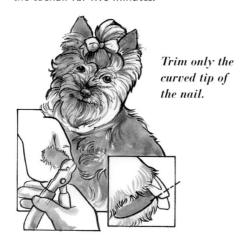

Trim only the curved tip of the nail.

Manicures

You can use baby nail trimmers (for human babies) to trim Yorkie puppy nails.

Replace dull blades so they do not break, shred, or crack the nails. An electric toenail filer does a nice job of rounding off and smoothing the nails after trimming.

When you are finished, be sure to praise Dickens for his cooperation. Without it, nail trimming is virtually impossible!

A beautiful Yorkie has the magical power to stop people in their tracks—and then steal their hearts. Yorkies are natural crowd pleasers. Wherever you go with your diminutive darling, he will be the center of attention.

Exercise

Yorkshire Terriers *love* to go on walks, and walking is one of the best forms of exercise for them. Yorkies also love to play games in the yard. Exercising Dickens means exercise for you, too!

Develop a healthful exercise program suitable for your Yorkie's age, stage of development, health, and physical abilities. A regular exercise program will strengthen Dickens's cardiovascular system, endurance, and function. Exercise will also strengthen his bones and joints, and develop muscles.

Do not take Dickens out for infrequent, strenuous exercise, especially if he is just a little puppy or a very old dog. Consult your veteri-

One of the best ways you can exercise your Yorkie is to take him on a walk.

narian and tailor a program suited to your Yorkie's needs.

Exercise Activities for Your Yorkshire Terrier

Walking: Walking is the best form of exercise for your Yorkie. Just remember that for every step you take, your Yorkie has to take several steps! A brisk walking pace for you can be full speed for a tiny Yorkie puppy. Don't overdo it. Start with short walks each day and gradually increase the distance or speed according to your pet's abilities.

Yorkie joints and bones are delicate, especially if they are young and still developing, or old and arthritic. Exercise on a soft, level surface, such as a lawn or the beach. Sidewalks and asphalt are uncomfortable and hard on the joints upon

impact. They are also very hot during the summer. Rocky or gravel surfaces hurt tiny feet.

Check the feet for stickers, torn toenails, cuts, or abrasions after every walk. If there are sores, treat them and discontinue walks until the feet have completely healed. If you live where it snows, don't let Dickens walk on salted roadways. He can develop salt burns. Carry him!

Always keep your Yorkshire Terrier on a leash when you are exercising him in public to reduce the chances of loss or injury.

Catch, Fetch, and Retrieve: Many Yorkshire Terriers will chase and retrieve objects for their owners. You can use a wide variety of interesting objects for this game, including flying disks, balls, and dumbbells. Just be sure they are small enough and soft enough for your pet's tiny, tender mouth.

Toys

Yorkshire Terriers love toys. They love to "shake and kill" them, too! Toys with flapping parts, or that crackle or rattle, are especially exciting. Be sure the toys you buy are durable and safe.

Chew toys are good for the gums and exercise the jaws. Some help reduce tartar buildup on the teeth. Chew toys are great distractions. They keep Dickens busy chewing on something other than your furniture and clothing.

Not all toys are suitable for Yorkies. For example, cow hooves, available as chew toys in local pet stores, are very hard and can cause tooth fracture. Below is a list of dangerous toys that can break, shred, or tear and become lodged in the airway passages or gastrointestinal tract.

Never leave your Yorkie puppy outside without supervision.

TIP

Homemade Toys

Sometimes the safest and least expensive toys are the ones you make yourself. A ball secured inside an old sock makes a fun toy that can be tugged and pulled in play. Two big socks tied in a giant knot make a toy soft enough to chew on but too big to swallow.

Dangerous Toys

- Rawhide sticks, bones, and other shapes
- Latex toys, rubber toys, cotton ropes, hard plastic toys
- Toys small enough to be swallowed
- Toys with small parts that can be swallowed (buttons, bells, squeakers)

Traveling with Your Yorkie

Yorkies love to travel, and no doubt a big part of the reason you chose this toy breed is because of its small, portable size. Surely you were planning on taking your Yorkie with you wherever and whenever you can. No matter where you are going—dog shows, running errands, or traveling the globe—Dickens wants to go with you. And having him accompany you makes every outing much more fun.

Travel Tips

1. Train your Yorkie to a travel kennel early in life. Put food treats and toys in the kennel to make it more inviting.

2. Make a few short practice trips, even if it's just driving around the block.

3. Make hotel, campground, and airline reservations well in advance and *be sure to tell them you are traveling with a pet.*

4. Make a list of everything you will need and pack early.

5. Microchip your pet and buy identification tags for the collar and harness.

6. Obtain a health certificate for out-of-state or international travel within 10 days of your departure date.

7. Make sure vaccinations are up to date. Check if special medications for the trip are recommended, such as medication for the prevention of heartworm disease or carsickness.

8. Make sure you have all the things you will need during the trip, including items in case of illness or emergency.

- Travel kennel
- Collar and harness with identification tags and leash
- Dishes, food, water bottle with sipper tube, and bottled water
- Medications
- First aid kit
- Toys and bedding from home
- Grooming supplies
- Cleanup equipment: pooper scooper, plastic bags, paper towels
- Veterinary records and photo identification

On the Road Again!
Traveling by Car

Yorkshire Terriers love to travel by car. To help prevent carsickness, limit food one hour before travel begins and, if possible and safe, place the travel kennel where Dickens can see out the window.

Tranquilizers are *not* recommended. Ask your veterinarian about meclizine (Antivert), an

Yorkshire Terriers love to travel. Wherever you go, your Yorkie wants to go with you. Be sure to bring along everything you will need for the trip, including your pet's favorite toys.

antihistamine that has been shown to be effective for some dogs.

Never leave your Yorkshire Terrier in a parked car on a hot day, even for a few minutes. Your Yorkie cannot tolerate hot weather. The temperature inside a car, even with the windows cracked open and parked in the shade, can quickly soar past 120 degrees Fahrenheit within a few short minutes, and your pet can quickly die of heatstroke.

Take to the Skies!
Flying with Your Yorkie

Your Yorkie's portable size makes it easy to take him on domestic flights. Dickens is small enough to board the plane as a carry-on and fit comfortably under the seat in front of you in his travel kennel or travel bag.

Your Yorkie must be able to sit, stand, turn around, and lie down comfortably in his travel kennel.

Most airlines allow only two animals in the cabin, so make your reservation as early as possible.

Overseas travel is different. Most airlines will not allow pets in the cabin for overseas flights. There are also special requirements for dogs entering foreign countries, so check with the airlines as well as the embassies of the countries you will be visiting to be sure you have all the necessary requirements and documentation in order.

Keep Dickens well hydrated during the trip. If he travels in the cabin with you, bring a small dish, a portable folding dish, or a water bottle with sipper tube, and offer him water frequently.

Tranquilizers are not recommended for air travel. Tranquilizers can be harmful, or even cause death, in dogs during travel at high altitudes.

Grooming Your Yorkie

A huge part of the Yorkshire Terrier's luring appeal is his stunning, long, silky, flowing, blue-and-tan coat. But that gorgeous gown wasn't created overnight. It is a labor of love and the result of excellent health, high-quality nutrition, the right genetics, and hours of regular grooming. Brushing distributes natural oils in

========

TIP

Grooming

Yorkshire Terrier breeders, professional handlers, and dog groomers can teach you many grooming techniques.

========

the coat and keeps it free of mats and tangles. To grow a beautiful coat, your Yorkie has to have very healthy skin, too.

Grooming should be enjoyable for both you and Dickens. If you don't like to groom, you shouldn't own a Yorkshire Terrier! Many Yorkie owners consider grooming a form of relaxation and artistic expression. It is a documented fact that people can lower their blood pressure simply by caressing an animal, so grooming should be beneficial to both you and your Yorkie's health!

Yorkies have very sensitive skin and can be prone to skin conditions and allergies. Grooming stimulates the skin, spreads natural oils, and gives you an opportunity to check Dickens thoroughly for signs of dry or oily skin, and for lumps and bumps, parasites, stickers, and scabs.

The more you practice grooming, the more skilled you will be and the more handsome Dickens will look. A few minutes of training and grooming every day will teach Dickens how to stand and lie down calmly on the grooming table and make the grooming sessions safe and fun for both of you.

Coat Quality

Your Yorkshire Terrier inherited his coat quality, texture, and color from his parents. Without the genes to grow a fabulous show coat, all the products in the world (shampoos, rinses, nutritional supplements, brushes, and combs) will not turn an ordinary coat into a champion show coat. There is no substitute for good genetics that can be purchased in a bottle at the pet store. A beautiful coat starts by buying a healthy, high-quality Yorkie from a reputable breeder. Then it is up to you to make sure Dickens's coat grows to its full genetic potential by giving him the best food and care that you possibly can.

Ouch! Protect the Skin!

1. Do not use harsh shampoos, chemicals, or products on your Yorkie's skin.

2. Avoid hot, dry environments that can dry out your pet's skin. Yorkies can develop itchy, flaky skin during the winter if subjected to heaters, radiators, and fireplaces.

3. Protect your Yorkie from unsanitary and damp environments that can cause skin problems such as bacterial and fungal infections.

Prevent Skin Allergies

1. Feed your Yorkie a high-quality diet. If he has food allergies, feed him a hypoallergenic diet. Ask your veterinarian for recommendations.

2. Give your Yorkie bedding made of natural materials. Some synthetic bedding and beds containing cedar shavings can cause skin allergies.

3. Check regularly for parasites, and treat them immediately before they get out of control. Flea allergy dermatitis (FAD) is one of the leading causes of hair loss in dogs.

Skin-Deep Hair Facts

• Healthy skin is absolutely necessary for your Yorkshire Terrier to grow beautiful hair.
• Yorkie hair does not grow continuously. It grows in cycles and sheds throughout the

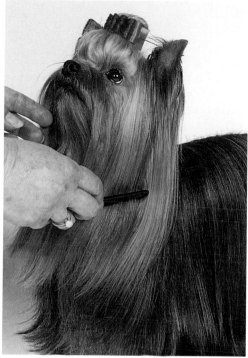

A Yorkie's beautiful coat is the product of regular grooming, good nutrition, excellent health, and lots of loving care.

year because different hairs are in different growth stages.

• Hair is made up of almost solid protein, called keratin. Thirty percent or more of the protein in a Yorkie's diet is used for skin and coat. *Without a high-quality diet, your Yorkie cannot grow a beautiful coat.*

• Most skin and hair problems are caused by poor diet, inadequate nutrition, junk foods, parasites, and food allergies.

• High-quality nutrition improves coat quality more than vitamins, supplements, and hair products.

• Yorkie coats grow about .1 to .2 mm each day. That distance multiplied by the hundreds of thousands of growing hairs on the body totals about 50 feet (150 m) of hair growth each day!

• Inadequate or poor diet can shorten, delay, or stop hair growth and cause faulty hair cuticles, dull coat, and hair breakage.

• Hormonal imbalances can cause hair loss or skin problems.

• Photoperiod (the number of hours of light exposure each day) affects Yorkie shedding more than environmental temperature does.

• Daily brushing is necessary to remove dead hairs, stimulate the skin, and distribute natural oils in the coat.

It's wonderful to come home and be greeted by your devoted Yorkie companion!

• Your Yorkie's coat mirrors his health status. If he has parasites, allergies, hormonal problems, or is sick, the problems will be reflected in his coat's poor appearance.

Make Grooming Safe, Easy, and Fun!

1. The sooner you begin training your Yorkie to be well behaved during grooming, the easier, safer, and more fun grooming will be for both of you.

2. Designate an area exclusively for grooming, in an easy-to-clean, convenient location close to an electrical outlet (for hair dryer, electric nail file, or vacuum cleaner).

3. Select a table that is high enough for you to work at a comfortable height.

4. Use a nonslip mat or table surface to prevent falls or injury.

5. Start by teaching your Yorkie how to stand and lie down on a grooming table.

6. Teach your Yorkie to allow you to handle his feet so you can trim the feet and nails. Gently lift and hold each foot for a few seconds until he becomes used to having them handled.

7. Be gentle and patient, yet firm. Make it a fun game and give food rewards.

8. Invest in the best. Purchase high-quality tools and equipment.

9. Place all the grooming items you need near the grooming table, within easy reach.

10. Use only products designed for use in dogs to ensure a pH balanced for canine skin, including emollient shampoos and conditioners.

11. *Several short training sessions are better than one long one.*

12. *Never leave your Yorkshire Terrier unattended on the table.*

Grooming Tools and Supplies

Have all supplies handy before you begin:
- Grooming table
- Nonslip mat and towels
- Brush with natural bristle (nylon brushes break hair)
- Optional brush with straight, flexible metal pins to be used carefully (Don't scratch or injure the skin! Avoid slicker brushes; they can hurt sensitive, delicate skin.)
- Metal double-side comb with wide-spaced and close-spaced teeth
- Rat-tailed comb (from beauty-supply stores), or a short knitting needle, to make partings
- Small hair bands (do not use rubber bands—they cause hair breakage—and do not use latex if you have a latex allergy)
- Scissors (blunt tipped)
- Nail trimmers
- Styptic powder or gel
- Spray bottle
- Detangling spray
- Emollient, premium, gentle shampoo (pH balanced for dog skin)
- Gentle hair rinse (for dogs)
- Tissue paper for crackering
- Oil (such as almond oil) for the coat
- Gentle ear-cleaning solution (available from your veterinarian)
- Ear powder or cornstarch
- Cotton-tipped swabs or cotton balls
- Towels: soft cloth and paper
- Soft washcloths
- Hair dryer
- Electric nail sander (optional)
- Soft toothbrush
- Dog dentifrice (do not use toothpaste for humans)
- Small sink or basin for bathing and rinsing

Crackering

Crackering is a method of wrapping sections of the Yorkie's coat in acid-free tissue paper to protect it and keep it clean and tangle-free. The tissue paper is folded such that a section of hair lies in the center and then the paper is folded, left and right, over the hair. The paper is then folded in half, and then in half again and secured with a band. The overall appearance is of little square paper "crackers" with a band across the center. Crackering starts with the top knot, then the moustache and chin, and finally the long hairs on the sides of the body. Ask a breeder or professional groomer to teach you how to cracker.

If you are not exhibiting Dickens at shows and find that a show coat is too much work, there are several Yorkie cuts that require less maintenance. You can trim Dickens's body hair shorter, so that it doesn't come in contact with the floor. Or, you can clip the top half of Dickens's coat, so that only the sides grow long. You can even clip all of the body hair shorter.

No matter what kind of "do" Dickens wears, grooming will always be an essential part of his health care.

Neat Feet!

Trimmed feet look very neat and prevent hair mats, dirt, grass awns, stickers, and excess moisture (leading to bacterial growth, moist dermatitis, and sores) from accumulating between the toes. Trimmed feet also prevent slipping and make walking and running easier.

Do not bathe your Yorkie until his coat has been completely combed and detangled!

Step 1—Check skin and hair.

Check the skin for redness, sores, and parasites. Check the hair for mats, knots, and tangles. If there are thick mats that must be cut out, take your Yorkie to a professional groomer.

Step 2—Wet the coat.

Using a water spray bottle or a coat detangling conditioner, *lightly* wet the coat. Brushing a dry coat can break the hairs.

Step 3—"Line brush" the body.

Place your Yorkie on his side, push the hair on the upper side of his body from the chest up over his back, and hold the hair in place with one hand. With the other hand, make a horizontal part and section the bottom portion of the hair in 1/2 inch (1 cm) increments. Separate knots and tangles gently, using your fingers. Brush the section of the hair, starting at the skin and ending at the tip of the hairs, then comb it. Part the coat to isolate another horizontal section of hair above the one you just combed and repeat the process.

Gradually work up, by sections, to the center of the back. Repeat on the opposite side.

Step 4—Brush the fall.

Divide the long hair on your Yorkie's head (fall) in sections. Brush and comb the sections.

Step 5—Clean the face.

Eyes: Use a clean, damp cloth to gently clean away tearing or discharge in the corners of the eyes.

Nose: Wipe the corners of the nostrils to remove dirt and discharge.

Mouth: Wipe the mouth to remove food particles, hair, and saliva.

Ears: Pluck excess hair from the inside of the ears to prevent accumulation of wax and dirt. Carefully clean the inside of the ears with a cotton ball and ear cleaner. Dry the ears. Now put cotton balls in the ears to keep out water during the bath.

Step 6—Bathe your Yorkie.

Adjust the water to a comfortable temperature.

Use a spray hose to saturate the coat with water.

Apply a premium dog shampoo and massage it over the entire body in the direction of hair growth. Do not use a cir-

cular massage motion, as this will tangle the coat. Start at the center of the back and work downward, to the sides of the body and limbs.

Make sure soapy water doesn't get in the eyes, ears, or nose.

Step 7—Rinse the coat.

Use comfortable, warm water and a spray hose to thoroughly rinse soap out of the coat. Cover your Yorkie's eyes and nose as you rinse. Direct the spray on the top of the head backward so that water doesn't enter the ear canals. Apply a conditioning rinse throughout the coat, soak, then rinse thoroughly with the spray hose.

Step 8—Dry your Yorkie.

Using soft towels, blot, don't rub, your Yorkie. Blot until dry. Keep your Yorkie warm. *Don't let your Yorkie get cold or chilled!*

You can also blow-dry your Yorkie's coat. Do not move the dryer back and forth over the coat. This causes tangles. Instead, dry a small area at a time, blowing in the direction of hair growth. Brush the coat in sections with one hand as you hold the dryer in the other hand.

Do not hold the dryer too close to the skin or keep it in one place for too long or you can burn your Yorkie's skin!

Step 9—Make a topknot.

There are several ways to make topknots. You can make a single topknot, on the top center of the head, or a double topknot, with a knot centered above each eye. You can increase the size of the topknot by putting hair gel on the inside hairs and back-brushing them, and then smoothing the top hairs over to cover the knot. Topknots require a lot of practice and patience.

Place your Yorkie on his belly and give him a soft pillow, or a rolled towel, to support under his chin so he can rest while you work.

Simple topknot: Part the fall horizontally across the top of the forehead. Start near the outside corners of the eyes, including hair on the forehead behind the eyes. Do not include the hair on the ears. Secure this section of hair with a band and center in on the head. Fold the hair section into a loop at the end so it can be hidden or tucked away with a band, bow, or barrette.

Double topknot: Begin as for a simple single topknot, then divide the hair section vertically into two sections, left and right. Secure each section with a band. Center the left section on the top of the head above the left eye and the right section above the right eye. Fasten each knot with a band, bow, or barrette.

Show topknot: There are different kinds of show topknots. Show topknots consist of two topknots. Make a front topknot. Make sure the band doesn't pull the hair on the ears, or on the corners of the eyes. Leave about 1 inch (2 cm) between the band and the skin to make sure it

Comb your Yorkie's coat before you bathe him. Comb the coat in sections to gently remove tangles. Give your Yorkie a soft towel to rest his head on while you work.

is not too tight. Make a second topknot behind the first one and secure it with a part. Comb both topknots together, combine them, and fold them into a loop. Secure the topknot with a band, bow, or barrette.

Step 10—Trimmings

Carefully shave excess hair from the front and back top one-third to one-half of the ears. Trim excess hair away from the feet with blunt-tipped scissors or electric clippers. Do not trim hair away from the eyes or nose. Lightly trim the moustache. Part the hair down the center of the back, starting at the base of the skull, and trim the coat carefully so it hangs straight and evenly on both sides of the body. Trim excess hair away from the rectal area to keep it clean. Trim the toenails.

Be careful not to cut the skin or foot pads with scissors or burn the skin with hot clipper blades!

To prevent serious injuries, never leave your Yorkshire Terrier alone on the grooming table or alone in the bath. Never allow your Yorkie to jump off the table or in and out of the bath.

FEEDING YOUR YORKSHIRE TERRIER

Your Yorkshire Terrier has special nutritional needs. She has a fast metabolism to fuel. Her diet must be high quality, highly digestible, and energy dense to make every bite count. Feeding your Yorkie a nutritionally complete and balanced diet is one of the most important things you can do to keep her healthy throughout life.

Every aspect of your tiny toy's well-being—from a healthy heart to her beautiful flowing gown—is affected by the quality and quantity of the food she eats. Fortunately, nutrition is one area of your pet's health care over which you have full control.

Your Yorkie has a small stomach, so she must eat small meals—and she must have several of them. Her stomach is too small to hold enough food in a single meal to supply her daily caloric needs and support her high activity level, especially if she is a young puppy. Jewel must have a good balance of protein, fats, and carbohydrates to prevent hypoglycemia (low blood sugar)—a common problem in Yorkshire Terriers.

Yorkies have special nutritional needs. Your Yorkie's dietary requirements will change as she grows, develops, matures, and ages.

Life Stages and Dietary Changes

Nutritional needs change throughout life. As Jewel grows, develops, and eventually ages, she will need different diets. For example, when she is a puppy, she will need a food that provides complete and balanced nutrition for growth and development. As she reaches adolescence, her dietary requirements will vary according to her needs and activities. When Jewel is an adult, she will have greater nutritional needs if she is active, doing obedience or agility work, on the show circuit, or being used for breeding purposes, than if she is a sedentary lapdog. Finally, as Jewel grows old, or if she is sick, she will need a diet suited to her health condition, such as a senior diet or a prescription diet.

Yorkie puppies must eat several small meals a day to prevent hypoglycemia (low blood sugar).

Starting Off Right

When you first bring Jewel home, continue feeding her the same diet the breeder was feeding until she has adjusted to her new family and home. A change in diet and feeding schedules during this important adaptation time can be very stressful for a Yorkie and cause stomach upset and diarrhea.

Your Yorkie has small teeth, a delicate mouth, and a tiny esophagus. Make sure the food is bite size—that is, Yorkie bite size! Feed your Yorkie food suitable for toy breeds. Don't feed kibble that is too large, too hard, too difficult to eat, or that could cause choking.

Take Jewel to your veterinarian within 48 hours of purchase for a physical examination and to plan a complete health care program. Discuss her specific nutritional needs. If a change in diet is recommended, make the change gradually.

━━━ TIP ━━━

Special Diets

There are prescription diets for several conditions, such as heart failure, kidney failure, urinary problems, and allergies. Consult your veterinarian.

For each of Jewel's life stages, consult your veterinarian to learn which type of dog food would be most beneficial for her.

Deciphering Dog Food Labels

There are countless brands and types of commercial dog foods available. Most claim to be the best food for your pet—but the truth is, not every dog food is good for Yorkshire Terriers. Yorkies need high-quality, energy-rich, highly digestible food.

Dog food comes in all sizes, colors, shapes, and consistencies (dry kibble, semi-moist, moist canned). The brands are packaged and named to attract *you*, the consumer. The challenge is to find a high-quality food that your Yorkie will *eat*. Yorkies can be fussy eaters and difficult to please. Other Yorkies may prefer junk food or inferior dog food formulations because they like the tastes and smells of the food additives and artificial flavorings.

The very best way to select high-quality dog food for Jewel is to consult with your veterinarian and Yorkshire Terrier breeders. You can also study dog food labels and select a premium dog food that provides *complete and balanced*

nutrition from high-quality protein sources.
Dog food labels are confusing and do not
always tell you what you need to know. For
details you must contact the dog food manufacturers directly.

Here are some definitions to help you inter-
pret dog food labels.

Ingredients

Ingredients include everything that is mixed
together to make the dog food. Fat, proteins,
carbohydrates, vitamins, and minerals are the
nutritional components of dog food. Non-
nutritional ingredients include food additives,
artificial coloring, artificial flavorings, and food
preservatives.

Dog food labels list ingredients in decreasing
order of preponderance by weight. In other
words, if the label lists beef, rice, and chicken as
ingredients, this means there is more beef than
rice or chicken in the mixture, and more rice
than chicken in the mixture. However, it does
not mean that there is more beef than rice and
chicken combined. It also does not tell you how
much more beef there is than chicken or rice or
what percent of each ingredient makes up the
total mixture. If beef is listed as the first ingredient, it is possible that there is only slightly
more beef in the mixture than rice. Finally, it
also does not tell you the quality of the ingredients. For example, unless indicated, you do
not know which beef parts make up the beef.

The list of ingredients tells you nothing about
the ingredients' quality or digestibility. Different
dog food manufacturers may use the same types
of ingredients, but the ingredients can vary in
quality. For example, if two different dog foods
list chicken as the main ingredient, the quality
of chicken may not be the same in each brand.

TIP

Wet vs. Dry

Yorkies are prone to periodontal disease
caused by plaque and tartar accumulation.
Dogs that eat moist, canned diets accumulate plaque and tartar on their teeth faster
than dogs that eat dry food.

Nutrients

Nutrients are necessary for life. Some nutrients, such as sugars, amino acids (the building
blocks of proteins), and fatty acids, produce
energy. Other nutrients may not produce energy,
such as water, oxygen, vitamins, and minerals.
The type and amount of nutrients contained in a
dog food mixture make up the nutrient profile.

Proteins

*Protein is the most important health factor
in your Yorkie's diet.* Protein is needed for
muscle, bones, growth, development, immunity
against diseases, and to grow that beautiful
Yorkie coat. Research has shown that one-third
of protein in canine diets is used for the support, growth, and maintenance of skin and hair.

High-quality animal source proteins are
better for dogs than plant source proteins
because they provide a better balance of amino
acids and have a high biological value. They are
also more digestible and produce less fecal
material and gas than plant source proteins.
Animal source protein makes up the most
expensive part of the diet.

Animal protein sources found in commercial
dog foods include beef, chicken, turkey, duck,

High quality protein is the most important factor in your Yorkie's diet. It is essential for good health. If your Yorkie does not receive enough high quality protein in her diet, she cannot grow a beautiful coat.

and of poorer-quality protein. *Meal* tells you the protein source is ground into particles (as in "cornmeal"). Meal may contain meat protein plus other tissues, such as organs.

Yorkies are carnivores, but they cannot live on meat alone. In fact, an all-meat diet is deficient in essential minerals (such as calcium) and other important components necessary for life. It is not a good diet for any dog.

Plant protein sources include soybean meal and soybean oil, and vegetables, such as corn. Corn is cheap, so it makes up a large component of many dog foods. Unfortunately, corn is fattening and also causes allergic skin conditions in many dogs.

rabbit, lamb, venison, kangaroo, fish, and eggs. Not all animal source protein is of high nutritional value. Look for the words *meat, meal,* and *by-products. Meat* means muscle, skin, and organs composed of muscle (heart, diaphragm) and skin, with or without bone. *By-products* include heads, feet, guts, liver, kidneys, brain, spleen, and bone. By-products are less expensive

Fats

Fats are important components of your Yorkie's daily diet. They add to the flavor of the food, provide energy, and play a major role in digestion and the assimilation of fat-soluble vitamins. The various fats (animal fat, vegetable oils, olive oil, fish oils) each have different effects on the body, and many are used for therapeutic remedies. Omega-3 and omega-6 fatty acids are important ingredients necessary for skin health and hair growth.

Carbohydrates

Carbohydrates are sugars, starches, and fibers. They are an inexpensive source of energy. *Researchers have not yet determined the exact amount of carbohydrates required in the*

TIP

Food for Fuel

A high percentage of protein in the diet is not the same as high protein quality. If the diet contains a high percentage of protein, but the protein is of poor quality, your Yorkie will not be able to digest or use much of it.

canine diet, yet carbohydrates make up the major portion of today's commercial dog foods, usually in the form of corn, cornmeal, rice, potatoes, wheat, or a combination of grains.

Dogs cannot digest fiber, so it is used (often in the form of beet pulp) in many dog foods to maintain dry matter bulk and for canine weight-reduction diets. High-fiber diets produce greater stool volume than high-protein diets.

Vitamins

Vitamins are classified as fat-soluble: vitamins A, D, E, and K; or water-soluble: all the B vitamins and vitamin C. Dogs make their own vitamin C and do not need supplementation in their diet. Vitamin E plays an important role in skin and coat health.

Vitamins must be correctly balanced in a dog's diet. Vitamin overdose is just as serious as vitamin deficiency. Both cause serious medical problems.

Minerals

Minerals are necessary for skeletal growth and development and muscle and nerve function. Among the minerals required for life are calcium, phosphorus, sodium, potassium, magnesium, zinc, selenium, iron, manganese, copper, and iodine.

Minerals should be provided in a balanced ratio. Excessive mineral supplementation can lead to serious medical conditions.

Additives and Preservatives

Additives and preservatives are substances added to the dog food to improve or enhance color, flavor, and texture, and to extend product shelf life. Additives, such as antioxidants, are added to dog food to help keep fat in the

TIP

Food Allergies

Many dogs develop allergies to corn, cornmeal, corn oil, wheat, and wheat gluten. These allergies often cause serious skin problems and digestive problems.

food from becoming rancid over time. Other additives are used to slow down bacterial and fungal growth.

Nothing is sweeter than a Yorkie puppy, but be forewarned. Yorkie pups are also very active, mischievous, and can be stubborn at times.

Chemicals

Many farm animals, especially chickens and cattle, are fed hormones and antibiotics. Grain crops are often sprayed with pesticides. The possible health risks associated with eating products treated with chemicals have long been a consumer concern. If the safety of these foods for humans is questionable, it is reasonable to assume that harmful chemicals could have an even greater effect on a Yorkie because of its tiny size and increased sensitivities. Ask your veterinarian about dog food brands available in your area that manufacture food from "organically" produced meats and produce.

Supplements

If you feed your Yorkie a high-quality dog food, vitamin and mineral supplements are unnecessary, unless prescribed by your veterinarian. By supplementing the diet, you can disrupt the nutritional balance you are striving to provide.

You do not need to supplement your Yorkie's diet if you feed her a high quality dog food. Do not feed too many treats. They can disrupt your pet's nutritional balance and also lead to obesity.

Always consult your veterinarian about any form of supplementation before adding it to your Yorkie's diet.

Homemade Diets

Do not try to formulate your dog's diet. Canine nutrition is a complicated field, and homemade diets usually fall far short of meeting a Yorkie's special nutritional needs.

Raw Diets

Do not feed your Yorkie raw meat, raw chicken, raw eggs, raw fish, or bones (raw or cooked). The bones can cause intestinal obstructions. In addition, your Yorkie can be poisoned by toxins from *salmonella* and *E. coli* bacteria found in raw meat and bones. Because of their tiny size, Yorkies can be more sensitive to these toxins than other animals may be, even in very small amounts. In addition, raw diets are not balanced and not nutritionally adequate for your pet's needs. Do not take chances with Jewel's health!

How Much to Feed

Yorkshire Terriers have high caloric needs and a fast metabolism, so ask your veterinarian to help you determine Jewel's nutritional needs, and don't rely on dog food label recommendations. Just as you would not eat the same amount of food as your next door neighbor, no two dogs are alike in their feeding requirements.

Yorkie Quick Reference Chart

Food Myths	True	False
Garlic kills intestinal worms.		✗
Garlic repels fleas.		✗
Brewer's yeast repels fleas.		✗
Onions repel fleas.		✗
Onions can be toxic to dogs.	✗	
Grapes, raisins, and macadamia nuts are toxic to dogs.	✗	
Some kinds of artificial sweeteners are toxic to dogs.	✗	

Yorkshire Terriers have small, delicate mouths. Your pet's food should be the right size and consistency for her to eat. Yorkies, like all dogs, can develop food allergies and may need special diets.

The amount you feed Jewel depends on the quality of the food you provide and her overall health, activity level, stage of development, and environment. If you feed a high-quality dog food that is easily digested, a smaller amount is needed than if you feed a mediocre diet filled with bulk and fiber material that cannot be digested.

The best way to know if Jewel is eating the proper amount is to check her overall physical condition. *You should be able to feel the ribs, but not see them. The ribs should not feel bony and should have a nice layer of flesh over them.*

When to Feed

Yorkshire Terrier puppies need several small frequent meals throughout the day to prevent hypoglycemia (low blood sugar). Their initial growth phase is during the first six months of life, although technically they are still puppies until 12 months of age. For each meal, make sure the food is available for at least 20 minutes. Some breeders prefer to feed young Yorkies free choice (also called "free feed" or *ad libitum*) to help prevent hypoglycemia. This

means food is available at all times and the puppy can eat whenever she desires.

If Jewel is a nibbler and not a glutton, you can feed her free choice from puppyhood through adulthood. *Always measure the food so you know exactly how much is eaten daily. If you leave food out during the day, be sure to discard old or stale food and replenish the dish with fresh food.*

Once-a-day feeding is never enough for a Yorkshire Terrier! Yorkies need several small meals throughout the day.

Yorkie Feeding Guidelines

Age	Feeding Schedule
Weaning to 8 weeks	Every 3 hours
8 to 12 weeks	Every 4 hours
12 to 24 weeks	Every 5 to 6 hours
6 months and older	Every 6 to 8 hours

Make sure your Yorkie always has fresh water available at all times. Feed your Yorkie out of a stainless steel bowl or a ceramic dish. Do not use rubber or plastic dishes.

Obesity

Overeating is the most common cause of obesity in dogs. More than 30 percent of the United States canine population is obese. Obesity is a serious health problem that can lead to heart disease, skeletal and joint problems, and metabolic diseases, such as diabetes. Fortunately, obesity is not as common in Yorkies as it is in other breeds and can be easily prevented.

The most effective way to prevent your Yorkie from becoming overweight is to monitor her food intake, avoid overfeeding, limit snacks and treats, and take her on daily walks.

If Jewel is overweight, do not put her on a crash diet and do not exercise her rigorously. Consult your veterinarian for a weight reduction plan and exercise program that are *safe* for her!

==== TIP ====

An Ounce of Prevention
Invest in a baby scale and weigh your Yorkie every week. If there is any weight loss or gain, discuss this with your veterinarian.

No Begging Yorkies, Please!
Prevent begging by

1. not allowing your Yorkie in the kitchen when you are cooking;

2. not allowing your Yorkie in the dining room when you are eating;

3. ignoring your Yorkie if she begs, no matter how cute she looks!

Water

Water is the most important of all nutrients. Water is necessary for life because it is needed for digestion, to metabolize energy, and to eliminate waste products from the body. Water makes up more than 70 percent of your Yorkshire Terrier's adult body weight. Dogs lose body water throughout the day, in the urine and feces, and by evaporation, panting, drooling, and foot-pad sweating. Water depletion occurs more rapidly in warm or hot weather or when an animal is active. Body water must be replaced continually, so Jewel must have fresh water available at all times to avoid dehydration.

A 10 percent body water loss can result in death.

Make sure Jewel drinks enough water every day. If she is continually thirsty or drinks more than usual, these could be warning signs for ill-

Special diets are available for Yorkies, based on nutritional needs, age, activity level, and health.

ness, such as diabetes or kidney disease. If she is not drinking enough, she will become dehydrated and can develop health problems. If you think Jewel is drinking too much, or not drinking enough, contact your veterinarian right away.

Food Allergies

Yorkshire Terriers can develop food allergies that cause itchy, reddened skin and hair loss. Hypoallergenic diets have been developed especially for dogs with skin sensitivities and food allergies. They may contain ingredients such as fish, duck, venison, eggs, potatoes, or rice. They do not contain beef, corn, or other foods known to cause skin problems in dogs.

Use stainless steel or ceramic food dishes. Plastic or hard rubber dishes can cause skin allergies and contact dermatitis in some Yorkshire Terriers.

Good Eating Habits
- Do not allow your Yorkie to beg.
- Keep track of your pet's daily food consumption.
- Feed enough to satisfy your Yorkie's nutritional needs.
- Do not feed your Yorkie food intended for humans.
- Feed only healthful treats and use them primarily as training rewards.
- Do not allow others to give treats to your Yorkie without your permission.

T I P

The Watering Hole

Your Yorkie can learn to drink out of a water bottle with a sipper tube. It will keep her moustache and facial hair tidier, too. If she drinks from a water bottle, you can easily measure her daily water intake.

KEEPING YOUR YORKSHIRE TERRIER HEALTHY

The best gift you can give your Yorkshire Terrier is the gift of good health care. A healthy Yorkie is more likely to live a longer, fuller, happier life. In fact, with excellent health care, your little companion may live well into his teens!

The best way to keep your Yorkshire Terrier healthy is to prevent problems before they start. Fortunately, preventive health care is easy. It is also better for your Yorkie, and less expensive for you, to prevent health problems rather than treat them.

Preventive health care includes regular physical examinations, good nutrition, immunizations against disease, an effective parasite control program, daily exercise, regular dental care, and daily grooming.

Selecting a Veterinarian

There are many excellent veterinarians from which to choose. Be as particular about select-

If you think your Yorkie is not feeling well, or is not acting normally, contact your veterinarian immediately. The sooner he is diagnosed and treated, the better his chances are for a speedy recovery.

ing Dickens's veterinarians as you are about choosing your own doctor.

Here are some guidelines to help you choose a veterinarian.

1. Find a veterinarian who is knowledgeable about Yorkshire Terriers and their special needs. Ask Yorkshire Terrier breeders, owners, trainers, and groomers whom they would recommend.

2. Make sure the doctors' location, office hours, schedule, and availability fit your schedule and needs. Do the doctors provide care on weekends and holidays? Do they offer evening and emergency services?

3. Meet the doctors and support staff. Are the doctors' assistants *licensed, registered veterinary technicians*?

4. Ask to tour the hospital. Is it clean, organized, and well equipped?

5. Ask about fees for services and types of payment methods available.

Start looking for a veterinarian BEFORE you need one.

Your Yorkie's nose should be clean and free of discharge. His eyes should be wide open, clear and bright, and free of discharge, redness, tearing, cloudiness, or squinting.

Yorkie Health Check

A home health check is a good way to detect a possible problem before it becomes serious. If your Yorkie is not acting normally, is depressed or lethargic, or not eating and drinking, contact your veterinarian right away. When illness strikes, your pet's condition can rapidly deteriorate. The sooner his problem is diagnosed and treated, the better his chances are for recovery.

Here are some things to look for when you examine your Yorkshire Terrier.

If your Yorkie has any problems, always contact your veterinarian immediately.

Anal Sacs

Dogs have two anal sacs, one on each side of the rectum. The sacs contain a strong-smelling, brown liquid. Anal sacs normally empty during defecation, because of pressure against the sacs. Sometimes anal sacs fail to empty, the brown liquid thickens or turns to a thick paste consistency, and the sacs enlarge and need to be emptied manually. If the anal sacs are plugged or impacted, they become irritated and painful. Signs of anal sac problems are licking under the tail, irritation and pain, scooting, and often a foul odor. If left untreated, the anal sacs can become infected or rupture. Take your Yorkie to your veterinarian right away for treatment and to learn how to manually empty the anal sacs when needed. Anal sac problems are common in Yorkies.

Vaccinations

Vaccinations are the best method currently available to protect against serious, life-threatening diseases. Anywhere you take your Yorkie—parks, rest stops, campgrounds, dog shows, obedience classes, your veterinarian's office—he can be exposed to germs that cause severe illness and possibly death. Although there is not a vaccine available for every known canine disease, we do have vaccines for the most common and serious diseases. No vaccine is 100 percent guaranteed effective, but if you are diligent about Dickens's health and vaccination schedule, you can rest assured he has a very good chance of being protected against serious contagious illness.

Vaccination is a medical decision, not a calendar event. The type of vaccination, and when it is given, should be determined according to your Yorkie's lifestyle, age, health condition, past medical history, and potential risk of exposure. Vaccination is a potent medical procedure with profound effect. There are significant benefits, as well as some risks, associated with any vaccine.

Yorkshire Terrier puppies are tiny and sensitive. Just to be safe, your veterinarian may separate the time interval between core vaccines, rather than giving them all at one time.

Yorkshire Terrier Health Check Sheet

What to Check	Normal Signs	Problems	Possible Causes
Attitude	Alert, happy, outgoing	Depressed, lethargic	Illness, injury
Appearance	Healthy, good body condition, glossy coat	Too thin, too heavy, poor coat condition	Numerous
Eyes	Clear, bright	Discharge Cloudy Squinting Redness, tearing	Infection, injury Corneal injury, cataracts Pain, sensitivity to light Irritation, allergies, trauma, foreign object
Nose	Clean, wet or dry	Discharge	Infection, foreign object in nasal passage
Ears	Clean	Odor, discharge, excessive wax buildup	Parasites, infection, foreign objects
Gums	Bright pink	Pale pink or white Yellow Blue or gray Bright red	Anemia, parasitism Jaundice Lack of oxygen Gum disease, heatstroke, poisoning
Teeth	Clean, white	Plaque and tartar, missing teeth	Periodontal disease, dental disease
Posture	Normal	Hunched	Pain
		Neck outstretched or sitting with elbows turned outward Drooping head Tilted head	Breathing difficulty Neck pain Ear pain, infection, ear parasites, foreign object in ear, or nervous system problem
Stance	All feet support weight equally	Limping, favoring a foot, shifting weight from foot to foot	Pain or discomfort
Movement	Walks and runs willingly and normally	Lameness, limping Skipping, hopping	Pain, injury, trauma, muscular or skeletal or nervous system problems, possible foreign object in foot pad Possible patellar luxation (slipped kneecap)
Skin and hair	Clean, healthy skin and glossy coat	Hair loss, sores, dry flaky skin, scratching	Parasites, poor nutrition, injury, hormonal imbalances, inadequate grooming
Under tail	Clean	Swelling, pus, open wound, odor	Anal sac problem, cysts, parasites

American Animal Hospital Association Canine Vaccine Guidelines (updated 2006)

Core Vaccines (Recommended)	Non-core Vaccines (Optional)	Not Recommended
Canine parvovirus (MLV)	Parainfluenza	Canine coronavirus
Canine distemper (MLV)	Bordetella	Giardia lambia
Canine adenovirus-2 (MLV)		
(Hepatitis)	Borrelia burgdorferi (Lyme disease)	
Rabies (killed virus)	Leptospira	

*MLV: Modified live virus vaccine

After the first year's set of booster vaccinations, your veterinarian will advise if subsequent boosters should be once every year, once every two years, or once every three years. Research suggests that vaccinations given once every three years are protective for some dogs. In addition, new vaccines may be available when you consult your veterinarian.

The table suggests guidelines only. Your veterinarian should customize puppy and adult booster vaccinations for your Yorkie based on your dog's health and specific requirements.

The vaccines your Yorkie receives, and the vaccine schedule, should be customized to your Yorkie according to risk, benefit, age, and health.

Guideline Schedule for Core Vaccines for Yorkshire Terrier Puppies

Vaccine	First Inoculation	Second Inoculation	Third Inoculation	First Booster
	Age	Age	Age	Interval
Distemper	8 weeks	12 weeks	16 weeks	1 year
Canine adenovirus-2 (Hepatitis)	8 weeks	12 weeks	16 weeks	1 year
Parvovirus	8 weeks	12 weeks	16 weeks	1 year
Rabies	12 weeks to 16 weeks (state laws vary)			1 year

Common Canine Diseases

Disease	Cause	Spread	Contagion	Symptoms	Treatment
Distemper	Viral	Airborne, body excretions	Highly contagious, especially among young dogs	Respiratory: difficulty breathing, coughing, discharge from nose and eyes Gastrointestinal: vomiting, diarrhea, dehydration Nervous: trembling, blindness, paralysis, seizures Skin: pustules on skin, hard foot pads	None. Supportive therapy only
Parvovirus	Viral	Contaminated feces	Highly contagious, especially among puppies	Gastrointestinal: diarrhea, dehydration, vomiting Cardiac: heart problems, heart failure	None. Supportive therapy only
Canine adenovirus (hepatitis)	Viral	Body excretions, urine	Highly contagious, especially among puppies and young dogs	Liver: inflammation, jaundice Eyes: "blue eye" caused by inflammation and fluid buildup Kidney: damage Pain and internal bleeding	None Supportive therapy only
Leptospirosis	Bacterial	Urine contaminated in kennels or from wild animals	Highly contagious	Kidney: damage and failure Liver: damage, jaundice Internal bleeding, anemia	Antibiotics
Parainfluenza Bordetellosis Both cause "kennel cough"	Viral Bacterial	Airborne, sneeze and cough droplets	Highly contagious, especially in boarding kennels and at dog shows	Respiratory: dry, hacking, continual cough for several weeks, may cause permanent damage to airways	Supportive therapy including antibiotics
Coronavirus	Viral	Feces	Highly contagious	Gastrointestinal symptoms: vomiting, diarrhea, dehydration	None. Supportive therapy only
Lyme disease	Bacterial	Spread by the bite of an infected tick or contaminated body fluids		Swollen lymph nodes, lethargy, loss of appetite, joint swelling, lameness, can induce heart and kidney disease	Supportive therapy including antibiotics
Rabies	Viral	Saliva (bite wounds)		Fatal, preceded by nervous system signs, including paralysis, incoordination, and change in behavior	None for animals. Post-exposure treatment is available for humans.

Parasite Control

Parasite control has never been easier! We have a wide selection of effective, easy-to-use products that prevent or kill internal (round-worms, hookworms, whipworms, tapeworms, and heartworms) and external (fleas, ticks, and mange-causing mites) parasites. These products are available from your veterinarian and require a physical examination, a heartworm test, and fecal examination, prior to dispensing.

Internal Parasites

Internal parasites (such as worms and proto-zoa) pose a dangerous threat to your tiny canine's health. They can cause diarrhea and, in severe cases, dehydration, malnutrition, anemia, and death. Take these internal parasites very seriously. What might be a light parasite load for a bigger breed of dog can be deadly to your

There are many excellent products available for parasite control, including products to fight fleas. Fleas are responsible for skin irritation and allergies, hair loss, and the spread of tapeworms.

Yorkie. Have your veterinarian check Dickens regularly for intestinal parasites.

Some canine parasites transmitted through contact with feces are also a health threat to people, especially children. Prevention is simple: good hygiene, a clean environment, and reminding children to wash their hands after handling animals and before eating.

Illness

Your Yorkshire Terrier may act tough, but if he gets sick, his health can take a nosedive very quickly. If Dickens is not feeling well, do not waste a moment. Contact your veterinarian right away. Early treatment makes all the dif-ference between rapid recovery and prolonged illness, or even death, for a little Yorkie.

Contact your veterinarian right away if Dickens has any of the following problems:

- Fever
- Pain
- Loss of appetite
- Lethargy
- Vomiting
- Diarrhea
- Coughing
- Sneezing
- Wheezing
- Difficulty breathing
- Difficulty swallowing
- Choking
- Limping
- Head shaking
- Trembling
- Blood in the urine or stools
- Inability to urinate
- Inability to have a bowel movement
- Severe constipation
- Dehydration
- Weight loss

Internal Parasites

	Mode of Transmission to Dogs	Mode of Transmission to Humans	Prevention
Roundworms	Ingestion of eggs in feces of infected animals, transmitted from mother to pup *in utero* or in the milk	Accidental ingestion of eggs from contact with infected fecal material	Parasiticides (products that kill parasites)
Hookworms	Ingestion of larvae in feces of infected animals, direct skin contact with larvae	Direct skin contact with larvae in soil contaminated with feces of infected animals, accidental ingestion of larvae	Parasiticides
Whipworms	Contact with feces	None	Parasiticides
Tapeworms	Contact with fleas and feces, ingestion of fleas, eating raw meat (wild rodents)	Accidental ingestion of larvae	Parasiticides
Heartworms	Mosquito bite	None	Parasiticides
Protozoa	Contact with feces	Accidental ingestion of organisms in fecal material	Parasiticides

*Health guidelines recommend repeating some internal parasite treatments quarterly. Consult your veterinarian.

External Parasites

	Animal Health Problem	Contagious to Humans
Fleas	Allergy to flea saliva, skin irritation and itching, transmission of tapeworms	Fleas may bite humans. Tapeworms also may be indirectly transmitted to people.
Ticks	Transmission of Lyme disease, skin irritation and infection	Humans can contract Lyme disease from direct contact with ticks. Always wear gloves when removing ticks from your dog, to avoid contracting the disease.
Sarcoptic mange	Skin lesions and itching, hair loss	Sarcoptic mange can spread from pets to people by contact.
Demodectic mange	Skin lesions, localized or generalized hair loss	No

First Aid for Your Yorkshire Terrier

Be prepared for an emergency. Put all your supplies together so you will have them on hand when you need them and won't waste precious time during an emergency trying to find them.

Make a copy of the emergency instructions in this book and put it in your Yorkie's first aid kit so you can refer to it easily. Keep your veterinarian's daytime and emergency telephone numbers, and the poison control telephone number, in the first aid kit. When you travel with Dickens, take his first aid kit with you.

Supplies for Your First Aid Kit

Basic supplies and materials for your Yorkie's first aid kit can be purchased at your local pharmacy or from your veterinarian.

First aid kit supplies:
- Bandage scissors
- Small, regular, blunt-tipped scissors
- Thermometer
- Tourniquet
- Tweezers
- Syringes (12 cc with curved plastic tips are good to flush wounds)
- Mouth gag (or small wooden dowel)
- Hydrogen peroxide 3 percent solution
- Triple antibiotic ointment (bacitracin, neomycin, polymyxin)
- Roll of gauze bandage
- Gauze pads
- Telfa no-stick pads
- Sterile dressing and compresses
- Sterile saline solution
- Elastic bandage (preferably waterproof)
- Self-adhesive bandage (Vet Wrap type)

- Activated charcoal (for treatment of poisoning)
- Eyewash
- Antihistamines (diphenhydramine or chlorpheneramine)
- Ophthalmic ointment
- Cold compress
- Muzzle (gauze strip will work)
- Blanket
- Paper towels
- Soap
- Sponge
- Exam gloves (vinyl)
- Penlight
- Flashlight
- Bottled water
- Pedialyte
- Nutrical (or other high-sugar product such as Karo syrup)
- Plastic bags
- Clippers (optional, but handy to shave wound areas)

The goal of first aid treatment is to give your Yorkie whatever emergency care he needs to save his life or reduce pain and suffering until you can contact your veterinarian. *Always muzzle your dog before initiating emergency treatment, for the safety of your pet and everyone involved.* Dickens may behave unpredictably when he is in pain or frightened. He may instinctively snap out in self-defense and bite you.

If someone else is available, save time by having the person contact your veterinarian for advice while you begin emergency treatment.

Yorkie ABCs: Airway, Breathing, Circulation

The most important things to check first in an emergency are the following:

1. Is the airway (trachea) unobstructed and open?

2. Is your pet breathing?

3. Is the heart beating?

• **Airway.** Your Yorkie has a tiny throat and very tiny trachea (windpipe). If his airway is obstructed, he can quickly suffocate. Removing foreign objects from a Yorkie's throat is difficult. Carefully open the mouth to see what is blocking the air passageway. Yorkies have delicate jaws, so be very gentle. Use a small gag to keep the mouth open so you are not bitten. Use a flashlight or pen light to look down the throat to find the obstruction. Be very careful not to push the object farther down the throat with your fingers. Forceps may be necessary to retrieve the object.

• **Breathing.** If your Yorkie is not breathing, you must act quickly and breathe for him, or he will suffocate. Open his mouth, and remove any objects, debris, or saliva. Gently pull his tongue out straight so it does not block the throat. Place your mouth over his nose and muzzle. Make a tight seal. Blow a breath gently into the nostrils and watch for the chest to rise. Then stop so air can be expelled. Repeat this procedure, blowing a breath every 5 to 10 seconds, as you are able, until your Yorkie breathes without

Wherever you travel with your Yorkie, take his first aid kit with you. Being prepared could make a life-saving difference.

your help. Be very careful. Your Yorkie's tiny lungs do not have much capacity. Do not blow too hard or you can overinflate and damage his tiny lungs. Check gum color often. The gums should return to a bright pink color if your Yorkie is receiving enough oxygen.

Note: Be careful! Do this procedure only if your Yorkie is unconscious or you can be bitten!

• **Cardiac.** If you cannot hear a heartbeat, or feel a pulse, begin cardiopulmonary resuscitation (CPR) immediately. Lay your pet on his right side. Place your hands on top of each other and gently press your fingers on the left side of the chest, slightly above and directly behind the elbow. Continue to press and release at a rate of one to two presses every second. Remember to also breathe into the nostrils every 5 to 10 seconds, as you are able. Continue CPR until your pet is able to breathe on his own and you can feel a pulse.

Bite Wounds

The most common wounds Yorkies suffer are bite wounds. When Yorkies suffer dog attacks, the injuries are usually severe. Wounds to the head, neck, chest, and abdomen can be very serious. Wounds that penetrate the body cavity are life threatening, especially if the lungs are partially collapsed or the internal organs are exposed. Immediate emergency veterinary care is needed.

If body organs are protruding from an abdominal wound, cover them gently with a warm, sterile, damp saline dressing. Do not push the organs back into the body. Rush your Yorkie to the hospital.

Consult your veterinarian immediately about any bite-wound injuries, antibiotics, and possible surgical repair. If a stray or a wild animal (such as a raccoon or coyote) has bitten Dickens, discuss the possible risk of rabies with your veterinarian.

Bleeding

Bleeding or hemorrhage occurs from injury, trauma, or serious health problems. Use a gauze or clean towel as a compress to apply firm pressure over the wound to stop the bleeding. If a large blood vessel in a limb has been severed, hemorrhage is life threatening. Keep pressure on the area and rush your Yorkie to your veterinarian or an emergency clinic.

Bone Fractures

Fractures are among the most common injuries Yorkshire Terriers suffer. Many fractures are caused by owners accidentally stepping

> **For ALL medical conditions and emergencies, contact your veterinarian immediately.**

TIP

Tummy Upset

Do not use Kaopectate or Pepto-bismol for treatment of gastric upset or diarrhea. Their formulations have changed and are no longer considered safe for animal use.

on their Yorkies, being dropped by children, falling off furniture, or being roughed up by larger dogs.

Signs of bone fractures include swelling, pain and tenderness, abnormal limb position or movement, limping, and crepitation.

Yorkie bones are tiny, and it is difficult to make splints for them. Make Dickens as comfortable as you can, place him on a soft bed, keep him calm and warm, and restrict his activity. Take him to your veterinarian immediately.

Burns

Your Yorkshire Terrier can suffer three kinds of burns:

Thermal burns—from fire, boiling liquids, appliances

Electrical burns—from chewing on electrical cords

Chemical burns—from a variety of chemicals (such as corrosives, oxidizing agents, desiccants, and poisons)

If Dickens is burned, immediately cool the burn by applying a cold, wet cloth or an ice pack to the area. Protect the burned area from the air with an ointment (Neosporin or aloe vera). If he has suffered a chemical burn, immediately flush the burn profusely with water or saline to dilute and rinse the caustic chemical

If your Yorkie is sick or injured, keep him comfortable and contact your veterinarian immediately.

from the area. Do not let Dickens lick the area or he will burn his mouth and esophagus with the caustic substance. Contact your veterinarian immediately.

Choking

Choking is treated as previously described in Yorkie ABCs, above.

Cuts

Cuts should be cleaned well and treated with antibiotics to prevent infection. Serious cuts may require sutures, so contact your veterinarian for advice. If the cut is not too deep, wash it with a mild soap and rinse it several times with water. Dry the wound well and apply an antibiotic ointment to it. If the cut is in an area that can be bandaged, wrap the area with gauze and elastic bandage to prevent contamination and infection. *Do not wrap the bandage too tightly. Change the bandage daily.* Consult your veterinarian.

Dehydration

Dehydration means the body has lost too much water. The most common causes of dehydration in Yorkies are vomiting, diarrhea, and heat exposure. A dehydrated Yorkie has also lost important minerals from the body.

Treatment for dehydration is the replenishment of fluids. If Dickens is conscious, offer him water to drink. Do not force water down his throat if he is unconscious or too weak to drink on his own. Doing so can cause him to aspirate water into his lungs. Keep a bottle of Pedialyte on hand for emergencies. Contact your veterinarian immediately.

Heatstroke

Heatstroke is caused by exposure to high temperature. Confinement in a car is one of the leading causes of heatstroke. On a hot day, a car parked in the shade, with the windows partially open, can reach temperatures exceeding 120°F (48.9°C) within a few minutes. Overexertion on a hot day can also cause heatstroke. Dogs that are old or overweight are especially prone to heatstroke.

Signs of heatstroke include rapid breathing, panting, bright red gums, thick saliva, vomiting, diarrhea, dehydration, and a rectal temperature of 105 to 110°F (41–43°C). As the condition progresses, the animal weakens, goes into shock, becomes comatose, and dies. Heatstroke can kill a Yorkie in a few short minutes.

If Dickens is suffering from heatstroke, you must lower his body temperature immediately, but not too quickly. A rapid temperature drop

Dehydration, hypothermia, and hypoglycemia are the leading causes of Yorkie puppy death. Make sure your puppy always has plenty to eat and drink, and keep him safe and warm.

can cause more problems. Cool your pet by repeatedly wetting him down with cool (not cold!) water.

Check Dickens's body temperature every three minutes. When the temperature has dropped to 102°F (39°C), stop wetting with cool water and monitor your pet closely. When he is conscious, offer him water to drink.

Heatstroke is a medical emergency that requires immediate veterinary care. Intravenous fluids and various medications to treat shock and prevent cerebral edema (brain swelling) are necessary to ensure survival. Contact your veterinarian immediately.

Hypoglycemia

Hypoglycemia (low blood sugar) is a common cause of death in Yorkshire Terriers. Yorkies are active and burn a lot of calories, so they need to be fed several times throughout the day (as often as every three to eight hours, depending on age and activity level).

Symptoms of hypoglycemia are drowsiness, lethargy, inactivity, weakness, and nervous system signs such as lack of coordination. If not treated immediately, seizures and death quickly follow.

Do not force food or liquid into Dickens's mouth if he is unconscious. He can aspirate and choke to death. Instead, rub a sugar-rich substance on the gums, such as Nutrical (available from your veterinarian) or Karo syrup (corn syrup). Hypoglycemia is often accompanied by hypothermia and dehydration. Wrap Dickens in a blanket, keep him warm, and rush him to your veterinarian.

Hypothermia

Yorkshire Terriers are tiny, and most do not have much body fat. Do not let all that hair fool you, either. The silky coat does not give enough insulation or protection from the cold.

Three Deadly Dangers: Dehydration, Hypoglycemia, and Hypothermia

The Yorkshire Terrier's tiny size, high energy level, and fast metabolism make it challenging for this toy breed to stay hydrated, nourished, and warm.

Dehydration, hypoglycemia, and hypothermia are the most common causes of death in Yorkies. Stressed, sick, very young, or very old Yorkies are especially fragile.

Treatment and prevention consist of fluid therapy, balanced electrolytes, nourishment to keep blood sugar from falling too low, and keeping your Yorkie warm.

Very young Yorkies are fragile and are especially sensitive to the cold. Once they start to lose body heat, they cannot regain it without help. Signs of hypothermia begin with shivering and progress to lethargy, slow heart rate, slow respiration, coma, and death.

Warm your Yorkie *slowly*! Rapid heating, or overheating, causes serious problems. Warm Dickens by covering him with a blanket. Leave his head exposed so you can watch him closely, and place him in a warm area. *Do not use an electric heating pad.* Instead, fill plastic water bottles with very warm (not hot!) water and wrap them in towels. Place the water bottles near, but not directly against, his body. Refill the bottles when they are no longer warm enough. Check Dickens's body temperature (rectally) every five minutes until it has returned to normal. Do not allow his temperature to rise above 101.5°F (39°C). Observe Dickens closely for signs of problems. Follow-up care is necessary, so contact your veterinarian right away.

Eye Injury

Eye injuries are extremely painful. Serious injuries can result in loss of vision, or even loss of the eyes. Injured eyes can be very sensitive to light. If Dickens has an eye problem, put him in an area with subdued lighting. Contact your veterinarian immediately. If rinsing is needed, use a commercial eyewash solution or ophthalmic saline solution. When you transport Dickens to the hospital, cover the travel kennel with a towel to help keep out as much light as possible.

Insect Stings

Most insect stings occur on the face, front legs, and feet. A severe allergic reaction can lead to facial and throat swelling, making it

"Bee" careful in the garden. Bee and hornet stings can cause severe allergic reactions.

difficult or impossible to breathe. In extreme cases, anaphylactic shock and death can result.

Bees leave their stingers in the skin, but wasps and hornets do not. If a bee stings Dickens, you can remove the stinger by scraping it gently in one direction with a stiff business card. If that does not work, remove the stinger with tweezers. Be gentle and try not to squeeze the stinger, or more venom will be injected into the site. Apply a paste mixture of water and baking soda or an ice pack to the stung area to relieve pain. If the offending insect is a hornet or wasp, apply vinegar to the area for pain relief. Later, you may also put a topical antihistamine cream around the sting site. Sensitive animals often benefit from antihistamines such as diphenhydramine (Benadryl) or chlorpheneramine.

Watch Dickens closely for the next two hours for signs of illness. If the swelling worsens, or if Dickens has difficulty breathing, starts to vomit, develops diarrhea, or loses consciousness, contact your veterinarian immediately. This is a life-threatening situation, and immediate emergency treatment is necessary.

Poisoning

Poisoning is caused by eating, or inhaling toxic substances, or by contact with poisons on their skin, mucous membranes, or eyes.

Signs of poisoning include restlessness, drooling, abdominal pain, vomiting, diarrhea, unconsciousness, seizures, shock, and death.

If Dickens has been exposed to poison, contact your veterinarian immediately. If the poison came in a container, read the container label and follow the emergency instructions for treating the poisoning. If the instructions tell you to induce vomiting, you can do this by giving 1/2 teaspoon of hydrogen peroxide 3 percent.

Activated charcoal is used to dilute and adsorb ingested poisons. You can buy activated charcoal in liquid, powder, or tablet form from your veterinarian to keep in your first aid kit. If you do not have activated charcoal, you can dilute poison in the gastrointestinal tract by giving milk.

Seizures

There are many causes of seizures, including trauma and poisoning. Epileptic seizures are common in Yorkshire Terriers. Epilepsy can be hereditary (genetic), or idiopathic (meaning the cause is unknown), or it can be triggered by other health problems.

Seizures may be mild or severe, ranging from a mild tremor of short duration, to violent convulsions, chomping jaws and frothing at the mouth, stiffening of the neck and limbs, and cessation of breathing. During a severe seizure,

The 10 Most Common Poisonings in Dogs

- Ibuprofen (Advil, Motrin)
- Chocolate
- Ant and roach baits
- Rodenticides (rat, mouse, gopher bait)
- Acetaminophen (Tylenol)
- Pseudoephedrine in cold medicines (Pseudofed)
- Thyroid hormones (overdose)
- Bleach
- Fertilizer
- Hydrocarbons (found in paint, varnish, engine cleaners, furniture polish, lighter fluid)

an animal is not conscious and can be hurt thrashing about on the floor. Dickens may seem to be choking during a seizure, but avoid handling his mouth, or you will be bitten.

Try to prevent Dickens from injuring himself during the seizure. After a seizure, Dickens will be exhausted and seem dazed. Place him in a quiet room with subdued light. Keep him comfortable and warm. When he is conscious, offer him some water. Contact your veterinarian immediately for follow-up medical care and to determine the cause of the seizure and how to possibly prevent another one from occurring.

Shock

Shock is a serious emergency condition in which there is a decreased blood supply to vital organs and the body tissues die. Blood loss, heatstroke, bacterial toxins, and severe allergic reactions can all cause shock.

Shock results in a rapid death unless immediate veterinary care—including fluid and oxygen

Continue to pamper your Yorkie through his senior years. He deserves it!

therapy and necessary medications—are provided. Signs of shock include vomiting, diarrhea, weakness, difficulty breathing, increased heart rate, collapse, and coma.

Snakes, Toads, Scorpions, and Spiders

Your Yorkie is a digger and an explorer. This means he can encounter danger anywhere—in the backyard, or in the great outdoors during a hike or on a camping trip.

Poisonous snakebites. Common symptoms of snakebite include immediate severe pain, swelling, darkened tissue coloration, and tissue necrosis (tissue death).

Urgent, immediate veterinary attention is necessary. If the bite is left untreated, the skin and underlying tissue may slough off (rot). The amount of venom injected (envenomization) cannot be determined simply by the appearance of the bite wound, but because Yorkies are so tiny, it takes only a small amount of venom to kill them. Signs of snakebite poisoning include weakness, neurological signs, respiratory depression, and shock. Without treatment, death can follow.

Toad poisoning. Poisonous toads in the United States include the Colorado Rim Toad and the Marine Toad. The most toxic toad varieties are in the southwestern desert, the southeastern United States, and Hawaii. If Dickens has come in contact with a poisonous toad, contact your veterinarian immediately.

Spiders and scorpions. The brown spiders (fiddleback, brown recluse, and Arizona brown spider) are found in the southern United States. There is no antidote available for their venomous

bites. Black widow spiders are found throughout the United States. There is an antivenin available for black widow bites. Scorpions may be found in the southwest United States.

The Senior Yorkshire Terrier

A Yorkshire Terrier is considered a senior citizen when he reaches seven years of age, although for many Yorkies that just might be the halfway mark in their lives. As Dickens ages, you may notice changes in his behavior, activity level, and physical stature. He may slow down, sleep more, or have problems with urination or defecation. Yorkies develop plaque and periodontal disease faster than many breeds, especially in their old age. Your Yorkie's hair coat may become thinner, the skin less supple, and warts and other skin growths may appear. Cataracts become visible, hearing may diminish, and your little friend will rely more on his sense of smell. Muscle weakening, arthritis, a reduction in organ function (heart, liver, kidneys), decreased resistance to disease, and even senility may occur. These are all signs of the aging process.

Here's how to keep Dickens comfortable in his golden years.

✔ Keep your Yorkie comfortable and warm.

✔ Provide a soft, warm bed.

✔ Take your Yorkie out daily for slow, easy, short walks on level, soft, nonslippery surfaces, and keep his toenails trimmed.

✔ Do not let Dickens try to jump on or off furniture or climb stairs.

✔ Carry your Yorkie when he is tired.

✔ Feed a diet appropriate for your pet's age, health condition, and activity level.

✔ Schedule physical examinations for your senior Yorkie every six months so you can detect any age-related problems early.

✔ If your Yorkie's eyesight is failing, or he is hard of hearing, try not to startle him. Speak to him reassuringly as you approach so he knows you are there.

Euthanasia—
Saying Good-bye

Euthanasia means putting an animal to death humanely, peacefully, and painlessly. Even with the best care in the world, the sad day will come when you must consider euthanasia for your beloved companion.

The decision of when to euthanize depends on many things. A good guideline is that if your little companion is suffering and the suffering

The Basics: Vital Signs

• **Heart rate:** You can take your Yorkie's heart rate in two ways:

   1. Place your fingers between your dog's ribs on the left side of the chest, behind the elbow, and feel the heartbeat.

   2. Place your fingers on the inside middle portion of either upper thigh. You can also place your finger in the groin area where the leg connects to the body. Count the number of pulses you feel in a minute. *Normal resting pulse is 80 to 130 beats per minute, depending on age and whether the animal is at rest or has just been very active.*

• **Temperature:** Take your Yorkie's temperature rectally. A digital thermometer is recommended. (Ear thermometers designed for animal use are available from your veterinarian or local pet store. They may be less accurate.) Lubricate the tip of the rectal thermometer and gently insert it a distance of about 1 inch (2.5 cm) into your Yorkie's rectum. Support your dog so he does not sit on the thermometer, and try to keep him calm.

   Normal Yorkie body temperature is 101.5 to 102°F (39°C).

• **Circulation:** Capillary refill time (CRT) is a good indicator of circulation. Press on the gums for a second with your finger. The gums should return to a bright pink color as the capillaries refill. *Normal CRT is two seconds or less.*

• **Respiration rate:** Count how many breaths your Yorkie takes in one minute. Respiration rate increases with excitement, heat, or difficulty breathing.

   Normal respiration is 15 to 30 breaths per minute.

cannot be relieved, or if the quality of life is so poor that the bad days outnumber the good days, then it is time to discuss euthanasia with your veterinarian. Your veterinarian can answer questions you have and also help you if you wish to find a pet cemetery or desire cremation services.

During this sad time, take comfort in the knowledge that you pampered your precious friend throughout his life and that you always made the best decisions regarding his health and welfare—even when you had to make the most difficult decision of all.

Selected Medical Conditions in Yorkshire Terriers

Every dog breed is predisposed to certain health problems. Here are some medical conditions seen more often in Yorkies, although many other breeds also share these health problems. If you purchased Dickens from a reputable breeder, it is likely that he will not have any of these conditions, but if he does, this chart will help you recognize the problem at the onset.

Dental
• Overcrowded teeth, missing teeth, retained baby (deciduous) teeth, periodontal and gum disease, hairs trapped between teeth. Bad breath, inflammation, sore mouth, reluctance to eat.

Eyes
• **Corneal dystrophy.** Opacity of the cornea, usually resolves in a few months, without treatment, in Yorkie puppies.
• **Dry eye (keratoconjunctivitis sicca, KCS).** Abnormality of the composition of tear film, leading to eye discomfort and visual impairment, can be caused by autoimmune problems.

Color Code for Gums

You can tell a lot about your Yorkie's health just by checking the gums.
• Bright pink: normal
• Red: inflammation, fever, heatstroke, possible poisoning
• Red specks or red spots: bleeding problems or infection
• Pale pink or white: anemia, hemorrhage or significant blood loss
• Blue, gray: insufficient oxygen delivery to the body
• Yellow: jaundice (icterus), liver problems
• "Muddy": very serious, near death in some cases
• "Tacky" or sticky to the touch: dehydrated

• **Entropion.** Rolling inward of the eyelid margin toward the globe of the eye. Eyelashes and tissue rub on the cornea, causing irritation and sometimes ulceration.
• **Juvenile cataracts.** Opacity of the lenses, vision impairment, or blindness. Hereditary.
• **Lacrimal (tear) duct problems.** Plugged tear ducts prevent tearing, causing dry, irritated eyes. Treatment: Your veterinarian can flush the tear ducts open to restore normal tearing.
• **Progressive retinal atrophy.** A degenerative disease of the cells of the retina, leading to blindness. Hereditary.

Skin
• **Short hair syndrome.** The long, silky hairs fail to achieve full length, or are shed before reaching normal length. Believed to be caused by a shortened hair cycle. Onset at one to five years of age. No treatment available.

Respiratory

- **Tracheal collapse.** Flattening of the tracheal rings causing a reduction in the diameter of the trachea. May be congenital. Suggested causes include cartilage defect. Signs are observed at an early age and usually follow activity, play, or excitement. If the collapse is in the cervical area, there is coughing and respiratory obstruction on inspiration (inhaling). If the collapse is intrathoracic (in the chest area), the signs are more severe during expiration (exhaling) or cough. Both types of collapse can occur separately or simultaneously. A characteristic "goose honk" cough is frequently noted. Retching and fainting can also occur. Treatment depends on each individual case and consists of rest, reducing stress, possible surgery, a wide selection of medications (corticosteroids, antibiotics, bronchodilators), and weight reduction if needed. Tracheal collapse is common in Yorkies.

Circulatory

- **Patent ductus arteriosis (PDA).** An opening between the aorta and pulmonary artery that fails to close after birth. PDA is common in Yorkies and is genetically inherited. PDA leads to left-sided congestive heart failure. Signs of PDA include a continuous heart murmur ("machinery murmur"), shortness of breath, and coughing. Females are more often affected than males. Treatment is surgical closure of the opening.
- **Portosystemic liver shunt (PSS).** PSS is a congenital problem in which there is an abnormal communication between the portal and systemic circulation. Yorkies are predisposed to liver PSS. The liver removes many toxins, including ammonia, from the blood. In liver PSS, blood that would normally flow through the liver is instead diverted and flows directly into the circulation, and toxins are not removed. Toxins build up in the body, causing encephalopathy and nervous system problems, liver damage, stunted growth, personality changes, depression, seizures, coma, and blindness. Signs of PSS are usually apparent early in life. When possible, PSS is corrected surgically by finding and tying off the shunt(s) to prevent liver failure and death. If surgery is not possible, the condition can sometimes be managed by a strict high-protein diet and medications.

Nervous System

- **Epilepsy.** Seizures.
- **Hydrocephalus.** Hydrocephalus is caused by cerebrospinal fluid buildup in the ventricles (spaces) of the brain, resulting in compression and brain damage. Signs include a domed head with wide-set eyes, open fontanelles, seizures, visual problems, abnormal eye movements, and learning impairment. Symptoms vary according to severity. Hydrocephalus is apparent at birth or by several months of age. Treatment is difficult, expensive, and not always successful.
- **Steroid responsive tremor syndrome (also known as little white shaker dog syndrome).** Nervous system disorder (first diagnosed in small, white dogs) that begins with head and body tremors that worsen with exercise or stress. The cause has not been identified but is thought to be linked to an autoimmune and neurotransmitter problem. Affected dogs respond well to treatment with immunosuppressive corticosteroids.

Skeletal

- **Atlantoaxial subluxation.** The second cervical vertebrae (bone in the neck) flexes dorsally, causing compression of the spinal cord and

Don't get behind on your grooming duties. Keep the hair out of your Yorkie's eyes, so you can check his eyes for problems— and he can see the world!

serious neurological deficits. Usually caused by abnormal development or degeneration of the atlantoaxial joint. Most common in Yorkies less than one year of age. Thought to be hereditary in Yorkies but also caused by trauma. Causes abnormal gait, neck pain, and death from respiratory paralysis in severe cases.

• **Elbow luxation.** Usually present at birth in some Yorkies because of failure to correctly form intra-articular ligaments during embryonic development. Limb deformities ranging from mild subluxation of the head of the radius, to severe bowing of the foreleg, to inability to extend the forelimb. Signs include inability to bear weight on the affected limb, pain, lameness, and abnormal gait.

• **Hemivertebra.** Abnormal development of the spinal vertebrae causing them to be wedge-shaped. Diagnosed by X-rays. Some Yorkies show no obvious problems. Others may have hind leg weakness, spinal curvature, or pain in the spine.

• **Legg-Calvé-Perthes Disease.** Necrosis (tissue death) of the head of the femur (part of the leg bone that fits into the hip socket) resulting in hind limb lameness in Yorkies between 4 and 11 months of age, pain, limited motion, and shrinkage of thigh muscles.

• **Open fontanelles.** "Soft spots" on the skull caused by failure of bones in the skull to close.

• **Patellar luxation (slipped kneecaps).** A hereditary abnormality of the entire hind limb, in which the patella (kneecap) slips out of place, causing the lower rear leg to "lock" and

produce a skipping or hopping gait until the knee slips back into its groove. The condition occurs at a young age, tends to worsen with growth and age, and may need to be corrected surgically to prevent pain, lameness, and degenerative joint disease.

Reproductive

• **Cryptorchidism.** One or both testicles retained in the abdominal cavity. Treatment: surgical removal.

• **Monorchidism.** One or both testicles absent. Treatment: none. (If one testicle is present, it should be removed.)

• **Dystocia.** Difficulty giving birth.

THE TALENTED YORKSHIRE TERRIER

Yorkshire Terriers are more than beautiful charmers. They are animated, intelligent, and competitive. Yorkies are showoffs. They sparkle in the ring. They are always in the spotlight, and they love being the center of attention. No wonder Yorkies always steal the show! So, let's take a look at some of the fun ways you can put your Yorkie's talents to the test.

The Well-Mannered Yorkie: Canine Good Citizen

Yorkies that participate in conformation and sports have to be obedient and well mannered, too. So why not get credit for good behavior? The American Kennel Club offers a Canine Good Citizenship award for dogs that can prove they have social etiquette. Some of the requirements for a Canine Good Citizenship award include politely interacting with a

Your Yorkie is bright and eager to please. From the moment he enters your life, he will start learning. How well, and how much, he learns depends in large part on your abilities as a trainer. Are you ready?

stranger (allow being petted and examined, remain with a stranger while you leave briefly); walking on a leash without pulling; obeying the *sit*, *down*, *stay*, and *come* commands; and behaving well around other dogs and people.

Dog Shows

Dog shows are a lot of fun for both exhibitors and observers. Dogs are judged on how closely they meet the ideal standard for conformation for their breeds. If Dickens is handsome enough to compete against the best of his breed, join the American Yorkshire Terrier Club and a local kennel club. These clubs will give you information on show dates and loca-tions, judges, professional handlers, canine

To succeed in competitions, Yorkies must sparkle and radiate self-assurance.

toward a championship do not compete. Judges at fun matches may be official AKC judges or a knowledgeable dog breeder or handler selected by the hosting club. You can prepare yourself and your puppy for a future in the conformation ring by attending fun matches. They can help you get over the jitters if you are nervous about showing, because in a big competition, you must handle your dog with confidence. Dickens has to have more than a happy, outgoing personality for the show ring. He has to sparkle and radiate self-assurance. A dash of terrier haughty arrogance is expected! Fun matches are a great way to meet other Yorkie exhibitors and learn from them. You can practice all aspects of a real dog show, from traveling to grooming to exhibiting.

Conformation

When Dickens looks his very best and you both are fully prepared, you can enter the competitive world of conformation. Be sure to pack everything you need in advance, get lots of rest, and remember it's all about showing off your Yorkie and having fun. The winner of the day depends on the judge, handling skill, and quality of the dogs in the ring on that given day. If you don't win today, don't be discouraged. Only one dog walks away with the top prize at a show. Next time it might be Dickens!

Under the American Kennel Club show regulations, there are two types of conformation shows: specialty shows and all-breed shows. Dogs are judged according to their breed standard, and by a process of elimination, one dog is selected as best of breed.

sports, and other activities. Clubs offer handling classes to teach you and your Yorkie the rules of the games and how to participate in events. Dog clubs also organize fun matches—dog shows where you can practice and perfect what you've learned before taking the big leap into a real all-breed or specialty show.

Fun Matches

Fun matches are just that—*fun*! They are hosted by American Kennel Club–approved breed clubs and conducted according to American Kennel Club show rules. Only purebred, AKC-registered dogs may participate. Fun matches do not count toward points for a championship, and dogs that have won points

• A specialty show is limited to a designated breed. The show is held under AKC rules and sponsored by individual breed clubs. Each year the Yorkshire Terrier Club of America holds an annual national specialty show.

• All-breed shows

As the name implies, all-breed shows are for *all* breeds. Judging is conducted according to AKC rules. In addition to best-of-breed winners, open shows offer the title of best in group (for dogs considered to be the best representative of their group) and best in show (for the dog selected as the best representative of its breed and group, compared with all other dogs of other breeds and groups).

Most dogs competing in specialty or open shows are competing for points toward their championship. A dog can earn from one to five points at a show. The number of points available depends upon the number of entries. Wins of three, four, or five points are called majors.

To become a champion, a Yorkshire Terrier must win a minimum of 15 points by competing in formal, American Kennel Club–sanctioned, licensed events. The points must be won under at least three different judges as follows: two majors won under two different judges, with some one or more of the balance of points being won under a judge or judges who did not award the first two majors.

There are five different classes in which a Yorkie can compete for championship points, and the classes are divided by sex:

• Puppy class (divided into 6–9 months of age and 9–12 months of age)
• Novice
• Bred by exhibitor
• American bred
• Open

Agility competitions are fast paced and exciting!

Male dogs are judged first in this order: puppy dogs, novice dogs, bred-by-exhibitor dogs, American-bred dogs, and open dogs. The first-place winners in each class return to the show ring to compete against one another in the winners class. The dog selected as the best male in the winners class is the winners dog. This is the dog that will win the championship points in the show. The male that placed second to the winners dog in his original class (that is, puppy, novice, bred by exhibitor, American bred, or open) is then brought in to join the winners class and compete against the remaining four dogs in the class. The dog that wins second place in the winners class is the reserve winners dog. If, for any reason, the AKC disallows the championship points to the winners dog, the reserve winners dog will receive the points. The same procedure is then followed, in the same order, for the females, and the winners bitch (who

From tiny puppies to tough competitors.

also wins championship points) and reserve winners bitch are selected.

The winners dog and winners bitch then join a class called the best of breed. In this class are entered dogs and bitches that have already won their championship titles. The judge selects either the winners dog or the winners bitch to be best of winners and finishes the judging by selecting from the group an animal to be best of breed. If the best-of-breed winner is a male, the judge selects the best bitch to be best of opposite sex to the best of winners. If the best-of-breed winner is a female, the judge selects a male for best of opposite sex to the best of winners.

At an all-breed show, judging takes place for each breed, and then each best-of-breed winner competes in its breed group.

The first-place winners of each breed group then compete against each other for the coveted title of best in show.

Obedience Trials

In these competitions, it's intelligence that counts, so count Yorkies in! If Dickens is easily distracted, he might not yet be ready for prime time, because obedience trials take place amidst noise, interesting smells, new people, other dogs, and countless exciting distractions.

Dogs are put through a series of exercises and commands and judged according to how well they perform. Each dog starts out with 200 points. Points are deducted throughout the trials for lack of attention, nonperformance, barking, or slowness.

Agility is hard work. After physical exertion and competitions, be sure to give your Yorkie a meal to prevent hypoglycemia.

Obedience trials are divided into three levels increasing in difficulty: Novice—Companion Dog (C.D.), Open—Companion Dog Excellent (C.D.X.), and Utility—Utility Dog (U.D.).

To earn a C.D. title, the dog must be able to perform six exercises: heel on leash, stand for examination, heel free, recall, long sit, and long down. To earn a C.D.X. title the dog must be able to heel free, drop on recall, retrieve on flat, retrieve over the high jump, broad jump, long sit, and long down. To earn a U.D., the dog must be able to respond to signal exercise, scent discrimination tests, directed retrieve, directed jumping, and group examination. The dog must earn three legs to earn its title. To receive a leg the dog must earn at least 170 points out of a possible perfect score of 200 and receive more than 50 percent on each exercise.

instinctive behaviors. The jumps and obstacles are adjusted to the size of the dog, and the events are timed.

Many titles can be earned. Titles in increasing level of difficulty are Novice Agility (NA), Open Agility (OA), Agility Excellent (AX), and Master Agility Excellent (MX).

Agility Competitions

Agility competitions are lots of fun and very exciting. They suit many Yorkies perfectly because they are fast paced and challenging. Agility is performed *off* lead, so before Dickens can participate in these competitions, he must obey basic commands very well, especially *come*. If Dickens races out of the ring in pursuit of other interests, he could be injured by another dog at the show.

In agility, dogs compete in obstacle courses, jump over objects, teeter on seesaws, cross bridges, run through tunnels, jump through hoops, and weave through poles. These activities complement a Yorkie's natural abilities and

Tracking

Yorkshire Terriers have a very keen sense of smell, and they love to use it. Yorkies excel at tracking. Find out if Dickens enjoys using his natural tracking abilities. Hide little treats around the house or yard for him to find. Make the game more complicated by creating a trail of treats, laid one to several hours in advance of the search, and gradually increasing the distance between treats. At the end of the trail, have a surprise waiting, such as a favorite treat, or toy, or *you!*

Tracking competitions use an invisible trail of human scent, which the dog follows to locate a glove at the end of the course.

Rally

Rally is less formal than obedience, although the dog has to follow commands. Exercises include heeling, turning, weaving, obstacles, sit, down, come, and other maneuvers, in no set pattern. Handlers can direct and praise their dogs while they perform.

The American Kennel Club offers competitions to accommodate owners with disabilities and dogs with disabilities. Rally is a fun alternative to agility open to all.

Freestyle

In freestyle, you and your Yorkie "dance" together. You select the music and make up the choreography and then take Dickens through various moves and tricks in time to the music. He can weave around your legs, jump over your legs, turn in circles, heel, walk forward and backward, and do anything else you train him to do. The variety and originality is limitless and depends on you. Judges and spectators watch you and your nimble canine perform.

Flyball

Flyball is a fast relay race. Dogs that play flyball are keen competitors. To participate, your Yorkie must be able to run very fast, catch a ball, and leap over low hurdles. Flyball is a team sport. Each team has two dogs, and two teams compete at the same time. When each team releases the first dog on their team, the dogs run down different but parallel courses, over four hurdles, and toward a box with a spring-loaded platform. When the dogs trigger their respective platforms, a ball shoots out from the corresponding box. The dogs catch their balls and race back down the course, back over the four hurdles. The second dog on each team is released when the first dog returns. The first dog team to finish the race wins.

Earthdog Tests

Yorkshire Terriers are not yet officially allowed to earn earthdog titles because they were not originally bred to hunt *underground*. This doesn't mean that Dickens wouldn't be good at this sport. In fact, Yorkies have proven that they *can* do it. If Dickens wants to tunnel and hunt underground, he will have to do it at home or informally at competitions. Remember that this sport can be hard on the coat and that it will be more work to keep the coat clean. You will have a lot more grooming to do if "going to ground" becomes a part of Dickens's sports activities!

Frisbee

Yorkies love to play Frisbee, and they are good at it. Just be sure to buy a small, soft Frisbee that won't hurt Dickens's delicate mouth or break his tiny teeth.

Pet-Facilitated Therapy

For those owners who love to do community service, pet-facilitated therapy is a wonderful activity. Your tiny terrier can make a big difference in someone's life. Sharing your Yorkie's affection and your time with others is one of the kindest things you can do.

Yorkie therapy dogs help people in many ways by visiting nursing homes, assisted-living facilities, rehabilitation centers, schools for children who are mentally challenged, facilities for people with disabilities, and senior citizen centers. During these visits, therapy Yorkies can do a variety of things, including quiet cuddling, sitting on laps and being petted, and entertaining by performing tricks. Yorkies can make people laugh and share stories and memories. Just petting a Yorkie can replace anxiety, sadness, and loneliness with laughter, happiness, and comfort.

Therapy dogs must be very well mannered, obedient, and clean. They must have solid temperaments and cannot be aggressive or shy. They *must* have the right personality for the job and they *must* love what they do.

Pet-facilitated therapy is an emotional and rewarding community service. If you think you and Dickens would make a great therapy team, contact a therapy dog organization (see Information) to learn what is required and how Dickens can become certified.

Much more fun to hug and cuddle than any teddy bear, many Yorkies work their miracles doing pet-assisted therapy.

Games

Yorkshire Terriers enjoy all kinds of games, from hide-and-seek, to fetch, to Frisbee (a small, soft Frisbee). Yorkies are quick, agile, and coordinated.

There is no limit to the fun and surprises you will have with your Yorkshire Terrier. Beautiful, intelligent, energetic, bold, versatile, and full of fun, the Yorkshire Terrier is everything a dog should be—socialite, guardian, hunter, athlete, traveling companion, and devoted friend—and much, much more! It's no surprise that this quintessential canine is the most adored terrier in the world.

Yorkies are delightful playmates that love to be involved with their family.

HOW-TO: BASIC TRAINING

To be a good canine citizen, Dickens must learn acceptable canine etiquette and to obey basic commands. Yorkshire Terriers are intelligent and learn quickly, as long as they are having fun. So make training a fun game, with lots of praise and enthusiasm for the slightest bit of progress.

Your Yorkie must understand that he is not the "alpha" animal and that you are the boss. Keep in mind that young Yorkies are easily distracted. They also bore easily and tire quickly. So make training interesting by keeping sessions short, ending on a positive note, and always giving generous praise along with some tasty treats or a favorite toy.

Say your dog's name, then say "sit." Then give him time to respond. If you hold the treat above him, the nose will go up and the rump will go down.

Training a Yorkshire Terrier begins the moment you bring him home. It is never too early to start. The sooner you start, the easier Dickens will be to train and the faster he will learn.

A basic puppy class, or dog training class, is a good way to begin obedience training. There are as many different training classes and techniques as there are dogs and trainers, but not all of them work for Yorkies. Talk to other Yorkie owners and trainers and visit classes, so you can decide which class is best for you and Dickens.

Come

Dickens must first learn his name in order to come when called and respond to your commands. You must get Dickens's attention before you can teach him, and you can do this with food rewards. Train Dickens in an area free of noise and distractions. Start by calling his name whenever you feed him. Use small tidbits, along with a lot of enthusiastic praise, as a reward throughout the day whenever you say Dickens's name and he responds by looking at you or coming to you. With time you can alternate between reward-

ing Dickens with food and praise, or with praise alone, or a game with Dickens's favorite toy. In a short time, your Yorkie will come to you when called, purely for the attention and love you give him. Of course, you can still surprise him now and then with his favorite food reward!

Sit

Use a table to teach Dickens to sit. Start by saying Dickens's name to get his attention. Then say, "*Sit.*" Use a happy but firm voice. Hold a tidbit of food above his nose. As his head goes up to follow the tidbit, his rear legs will bend so his hindquarters drop. Give him a treat. If he jumps up or stands up, don't reward him. In the beginning you may apply gentle pressure on the rump to show Dickens how to sit and give him a treat and lots of praise when he does. Always say his name first to get his attention. Then say "*Sit*" and give him a few seconds to respond. Eventually replace the food reward with praise alone.

Down

Use a table to teach Dickens the *down* command. Start Dickens from a sitting position, say his name, and say "*Down*." At the same time, show him a food reward, near the table surface and below his nose. He will lower his head to eat it. Repeat the process and hold the treat slightly lower, just below the tabletop, so Dickens must bend his elbows and lower his body to reach it. The *down* command takes time to learn, but you will use it often for grooming your Yorkie. As you teach Dickens, you may have to gently and briefly hold him in position so he understands the command, but *don't* force him into position.

Stay

Stay is an important command. It could save your Yorkie's life. To prevent injury, don't use the table for this command. Your Yorkie may try to jump off the table to follow you and be hurt. Start by placing Dickens in the sit position and say "*Stay*." Don't use Dickens's name or he will try to come to you. Wait a few seconds, then say, "OK," and give a food reward and praise. The word *OK* lets him know he completed the task. Gradually extend the length of time Dickens must sit to 10 or 15 seconds, then 30 seconds. When he is older, Dickens will be able to *stay* for longer periods.

Leash Training

When your Yorkie comes when called and follows you, you can begin leash training. Begin by attaching a light line, such as string or yarn, to his collar and let him drag it behind him and play with it. Let Dickens follow you around with the string dangling along. When he is used to the string, replace it with a light leash. Dickens will quickly adapt to the leash dragging on the ground, and when he has, you can pick it up and walk with him. Begin by following Dickens wherever he goes. Do not pull on his neck.

The "stay" command could save your Yorkie's life. With training, you can gradually teach your Yorkie to stay in place for longer periods of time.

Next, hold the leash and encourage Dickens to follow you a short distance. Don't drag or pull on him, but don't let him wander away. If he walks with you, then stops, coax him back to you and give him a food reward for coming to you. Dickens will quickly learn that there is no resistance if he stays close to you. As soon as you resume walking, praise him and end the training session with more praise, a cuddle, and a food reward.

When leash training your Yorkie, do not pull on his neck. Encourage him to accompany you and reward him with praise and a small food treat as he improves.

Kennel and Breed Clubs

Yorkshire Terrier Club of America
Janet Jackson, President
P.O. Box 265
Saint Peters, PA 19470-0265
www.ytca.org

Yorkshire Terrier Club of America
　Foundation
Mary Trimble, President
P.O. 100687
Arlington, VA 22210
(703) 312-8832
http://www.ytca.org/foundation

American Kennel Club (AKC)
Registrations
5580 Centerview Drive
Raleigh, NC 27606-3390
(919) 233-9767
www.akc.org

Association of Pet Dog Trainers
150 Executive Center Dr., Box 35
Greenville, SC 29615
(800) 738-3647
www.apdt.com

United States Dog Agility Association
P.O. Box 850955
Richardson, TX 75085-8955
(972) 487-2200
Fax: (214) 503-0161
E-mail: *info@usdaa.com*
www.usdaa.com

Therapy Dog Organizations

Therapy Dogs International
88 Bartley Road
Flanders, NJ 07836
(973) 252-9800
www.tdi-dog.org

Health-related Associations and Foundations

American Kennel Club
AKC Canine Health Foundation
251 W. Garfield Road
Aurora, OH 44202
(216) 995-0806
akchf@aol.com

American Society for the Prevention of
　Cruelty to Animals (ASPCA)
424 East 92nd Street
New York, NY 10128-6804
(212) 876-7700
www.aspca.org

American Veterinary Medical Association
　(AVMA)
930 North Meacham Road
Schaumberg, IL 60173
www.avma.org

Veterinary Medical Data Base (VMDB) and
　Canine Eye Registration Foundation (CERF)
VMDB/CERF
P.O. Box 3007
Urbana, IL 61803-3007
(217) 693-4800
Fax: (217) 693-4801
http://www.vmdb.org/contactinfo

It's wonderful to be greeted by your devoted pet.

International Canine Semen Bank
P.O. Box 651
Sandy, OR 97055
(503) 663–7031
www.ik9sb.com

International Canine Semen Bank—San Diego
P.O. Box 668
Lakeside, CA 92040
(619) 654–4520
www.sharonvanderlip.com

Lost Pet Registries
The American Kennel Club (AKC)
AKC Companion Recovery
E-mail: *found@akc.org*
www.akc.org/car.htm

AVID
(800) 434–2843
www.avidmicrochip.com

Periodicals
The American Kennel Club Gazette
51 Madison Avenue
New York, NY 10010

Dog Fancy
Subscription Division
P.O. Box 53264
Boulder, CO 80323–3264
(303) 786–7306/666–8504
www.dogfancy.com

Dog World
29 North Whacker Drive
Chicago, IL 60606
(312) 726–2802

Books
The Complete Dog Book, Official Publication of the American Kennel Club. New York: Howell Book House, 1992.

Coile, D. Caroline. *The Yorkshire Terrier Handbook.* Hauppauge, NY: Barron's Educational Series, Inc. 2003.

Gordon, Joan. *The New Complete Yorkshire Terrier.* New York: Howell, 1993.

Haynes, Richard. *Living with a Yorkshire Terrier.* Hauppauge, NY: Barron's Educational Series, Inc., 2003.

Jackson, Janet. *A New Owner's Guide to Yorkshire Terriers.* Neptune City, NJ: TFH, 1996.

Linzy, Jan. *Yorkshire Terrier Champions, 1984–2001.* Incline Village, NV: Camino Books, 2003.

Palika, Liz. *Complete Idiot's Guide to Yorkshire Terriers.* Alpha, 2003.

About the Author

Sharon Vanderlip, D.V.M., has provided veterinary care to domestic and exotic animal species for 30 years. She is the author of several books on dog breeds and animal care and numerous articles in scientific and veterinary journals. She also is a regular writer for dog and pet magazines for general reading audiences.

Dr. Vanderlip served as clinical veterinarian for the University of California at San Diego School of Medicine and collaborated on reproductive research projects with the Zoological Society of San Diego. She is former chief of veterinary services for the National Aeronautics and Space Administration (NASA). Dr. Vanderlip is director of the International Canine Semen Bank ICSB–San Diego. Her practice focuses primarily on canine medicine, surgery, and reproduction. She gives seminars at kennel clubs and veterinary associations throughout the United States and Europe and is the recipient of various awards for her writing and dedication to animal health. Dr. Vanderlip may be contacted at www.sharonvanderlip.com.

Important Note

This book is concerned with selecting, keeping, and raising Yorkshire Terriers. The publisher and the author think it is important to point out that the advice and information for Yorkshire Terrier maintenance apply to healthy, normally developed animals with good dispositions obtained from a reputable source. Anyone who acquires an adult dog or one from an animal shelter must consider that the animal may have behavioral problems and may, for example, bite without any visible provocation. Such anxiety biters are dangerous for the owner as well as the general public.

Caution is further advised in the association of children with dogs, in meetings with other dogs, and in exercising the dog without a leash. Even well-behaved and carefully supervised dogs sometimes do damage to property or cause accidents. It is in the owner's interest to be adequately insured against such eventualities, and we strongly urge all dog owners to purchase a liability policy that covers the dog.

Extraordinary efforts have been made by the author and the publisher to ensure that treatment recommendations are precise and in agreement with standards accepted at the time of publication. If your dog exhibits any signs of illness, you should consult a veterinarian immediately.

The author and publisher assume no responsibility for and make no warranty with respect to the results that may be obtained from procedures cited. Neither the author nor the publisher shall be liable for any damage resulting from reliance on any information contained herein, whether with respect to procedures, or by reason of any misstatement, error, or omission contained in this work.

Acknowledgments

Once again, I am greatly indebted to my husband, Jack Vanderlip, D.V.M., for his invaluable help as an expert veterinary consultant and evaluator—and for taking care of everything at home and practice so I could again be free to write another book. Without his enormous help, this book would still be "a work in progress." A great big thank-you also goes to my wonderful editor, Kathleen Ganteaume, for her help, guidance, and professionalism.

Photo Credits

Isabelle Francais: pages 2–3, 4, 5, 8, 13, 14, 15, 19, 20, 21, 27, 30, 32, 34 (top), 36, 39, 41, 44, 45, 47, 53, 54, 56, 60, 62, 64, 66, 74, 81, 86, 89 (bottom); Pets by Paulette: pages 9, 11, 12, 22, 24, 31, 34 (bottom), 35, 37, 48, 52, 57, 59, 61, 63, 82, 83, 84, 89 (top), 93; Tara Darling: pages 17, 18, 23, 40, 58, 68, 71, 73, 75, 77; Kent Dannen: pages 6, 43; Shirley Fernandez: pages 85, 87; Norvia Behling: page 29.

Cover Photos

Front cover and inside back cover: Isabelle Francais; Back cover and inside front cover: Pets by Paulette.

All inquiries should be addressed to:
Barron's Educational Series, Inc.
250 Wireless Boulevard
Hauppauge, NY 11788
www.barronseduc.com

ISBN-13: 978-0-7641-3718-1
ISBN-10: 0-7641-3718-2

Library of Congress Catalog Card No. 2007005007

Library of Congress Cataloging-in-Publication Data
Vanderlip, Sharon Lynn.
 Yorkshire terriers : everything about purchase, care, grooming, health, nutrition, care, and training / Sharon L. Vanderlip ; filled with full color photographs ; illustrations by Pam Tanzey.
  p. cm.
 Includes index.
 ISBN-13: 978-0-7641-3718-1 (alk. paper)
 ISBN-10: 0-7641-3718-2 (alk. paper)
 1. Yorkshire Terrier. I. Title.

SF429.Y6V36 2007
636.76—dc22   2007005007

Printed in China
9 8 7 6 5 4 3